Hans W. Hannau
With revisions by William Zuill

THE *Bermuda* ISLES

IN FULL COLOR

Macmillan Press Ltd / Bermuda Bookstore Ltd

This edition published 1994

Published by THE MACMILLAN PRESS LTD
London and Basingstoke
*Associated companies and representatives in Accra,
Auckland, Delhi, Dublin, Gaborone, Hamburg, Harare,
Hong Kong, Kuala Lumpur, Lagos, Manzini, Melbourne,
Mexico City, Nairobi, New York, Singapore, Tokyo.*

ISBN 0–333–57598–9

Printed in Hong Kong

A catalogue record for this book is available from the
British Library.

The authors and publishers acknowledge with thanks the
following photographic sources:
M Emmerson (front cover, pp26, 74, 76 top)
Marriott's Castle Harbour Hotel (p86)
All other photographs are courtesy of the author.
The publishers have made every effort to trace the copyright
holders but if they have overlooked any, they will be pleased
to make the necessary arrangements at the first opportunity.

This book is a popular edition of the larger *BERMUDA in Full Colour*

DISTRIBUTED in BERMUDA by BERMUDA BOOKSTORE – BAXTERS LTD

INTRODUCTION

Visiting Bermuda is rather like visiting a Sóuth Sea island in the North Atlantic. The island is not one but about 138 islands, large and small. Altogether they comprise a little more than twenty square miles. Though the islands are in the blue North Atlantic, palm trees grow there and it never snows or freezes. The people don't wear grass skirts there, but the islands have inspired Bermuda shorts, a symbol of informality. Bermuda has its own style of architecture, represented by delightful houses with steep white roofs and with walls that are either white or tinted pastel. These island houses, literally cut from the rock, are now influencing the residential architecture of tropical and subtropical resorts thousands of miles away.

Geographically isolated, and tiny in size, how did this «coral chip of England» reach the prominence it enjoys today as one of the most idyllic islands in the world? What is there about Bermuda that attracts over 600,000 visitors a year from the United States, Canada, England, Continental Europe and elsewhere? And how do the inhabitants live where there are almost no industries, no mining, no raw materials and very little agriculture?

Some of the answers to these questions are to be found in Bermuda's natural beauty and some in the native charm which has developed along with Bermuda's history.

Bermuda is the first great modern resort island in the Atlantic and Caribbean area. It has perfected the art of being kind to strangers over many generations – indeed, since shipwrecked colonists came ashore in 1609. It has never forgotten the gallant seafarers who made it the greatest training ground for sailors the world has ever known, even greater than the home of the forefathers of the first Bermudians, England. Bermuda sloops were the fastest in the world in the great days of sail.

Bermuda is a land of contrasts. The fragrance of roses and lilies is laced with salt air. Though more than 600,000 visitors come to the islands annually, there still are lonely and magnificent coves where a solitary can find peace. The most modern amenities are found in the many fine hotels, clubs, and cottage colonies. Here also are small streets winding through a seventeenth-century settlement, and old forts built to defend against the Spanish and the French.

Golfing, swimming, searching for sunken treasure are only a few of the pleasures Bermuda offers. In addition to exploring the beaches and the looping coves and sounds along the shores, one can explore underground, for nowhere in the world are there more magnificent big caverns per acre. Many are lighted to allow the public to enjoy their beauty. Diving down to the colorful gardens of the coral reefs that surround Bermuda is an unforgettable experience. Bermuda is frequently used by scientists of many nations for underwater experiments.

The climate, which is idyllic, draws people to Bermuda where winter never comes. The serene pace of life on the islands and the wide variety of ways to rest and relax bring visitors back again and again.

HISTORY

Bermuda emerges into history with a reputation for being enchanted and mysterious. A Spanish seafarer, Juan de Bermúdez, gave his name to the isolated group of little islands in the mid-Atlantic. He sailed by them or was wrecked upon them, and the date of his discovery was 1505 or 1506, according to the most recent research. On a map of the Atlantic and its islands in Peter Martyr's **Legatio Babylonica,** published in 1511, «La Bermuda» was shown. On a high cliff called Spanish Rock on the south shore is cut a cross, the letters «T» and «F» now almost worn away, and the date 1543. Their origin is unknown. An English sea captain, Henry May, was wrecked here in 1593, and when he returned to England he gave an account of the islands.

The reefs round Bermuda were probably responsible for the wreckage of other adventurers of the sixteenth century, for in Queen Elizabeth's time the islands had achieved a reputation for being devil-haunted, mysterious, evil, and enchanted. Navigators avoided them like the plague. It was therefore a grand surprise to the shipwrecked party that landed in 1609 to find that they were lovely islands, with herds of wild pigs, fine cedar timber, nourishing plants, and a delightful, frostfree climate.

The landing was hair-raising. In that year a fleet loaded with food, other supplies, and colonists was sent out to bring relief to Jamestown, England's first settlement in America. The admiral of the fleet was

Sir George Somers, who began his seafaring career as a buccaneer, acquiring wealth and knighthood through the Spanish prizes he captured.

The Virginia Company put him in command of a relief fleet of seven tall ships and two pinnaces. His 300-ton flagship, the **Sea Venture,** was the largest ship that sailed from Plymouth to aid Jamestown.

Sir George Somers' Map of Bermuda

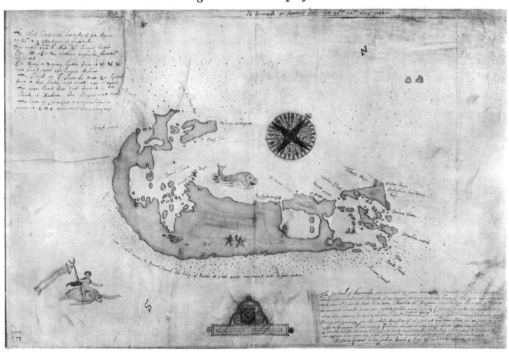

THE TEMPEST

The storm that struck the fleet is immortalized in Shakespeare's **The Tempest.** After seven weeks at sea, the **Sea Venture** lost sight of the rest of the fleet. The winds howled for three days and nights, and the ship, leaking heavily, had nearly sunk when land was sighted on the morning of July 28, 1609. Sir George steered his ship toward shore, for though he recognized that the land must be the devil-haunted Bermudas, devils were to be preferred to storms at that point. An account of the adventures of those men, women, and children shipwrecked on Bermuda was written by William Strachey, the secretary-elect of Virginia, and was later widely read in England. It is considered that this story inspired Shakespeare.

Strachey wrote: «...a dreadfull storme and hideous began to blow from out the north-east, which swelling, and roaring as it were by fits, some houres with more violence than others, at length did beat all light from heaven, which like a hell of darkenesse turned blacke upon us, so much the fuller of horror... surely as death comes not so elvish and painfull as at sea... our clamours dround in the windes, and the windes in thunder... The sea swelled above the clouds, and gave battell unto Heaven. It could not be said to raine, the waters like whole rivers did flood in the ayre. The glut of water was no sooner a little emptied and qualified, but instantly the windes (as having gotten, their mouths now free, and at liberty) spake more loud, and grew more tumultuous and malignant.»

The seams of the **Sea Venture** opened and everyone took turns working the pumps and bailing with buckets, including Admiral Somers and the Governor, Sir Thomas Gates. Finally the ship crunched between two rocks and was fast lodged and locked. The hundred and fifty men, women, and children were taken to shore in the long-boat and skiff, and they found themselves on «the dreaded islands of Bermuda... called commonly the Devils Islands [which] are feared and avoided of all sea travellers alive, above any other place in the world», according to Strachey. The spot where the ship went aground off the eastern end of Bermuda is called Sea Venture Flat. Sir Thomas Gates was in the first boat-load of survivors to reach the shore, and he named the spot where they landed Gates' Bay.

THE WEALTH OF BERMUDA

They found on the dreaded islands a wealth of food and beauty. Strachey wrote that Admiral Somers took so many fish in half an hour that they sufficed the whole company for one day.

«The fish are so good as these parts of the world afford not the like; which being for the most part unknown to us, each man gave them names as they best liked. As one kind they called rock fish, another groopers, others porgy fish, hogge fish, angel fish, cavallyes, yellow tayles, Spanisk makarell, mullets, breame, conny fish, morrayers, sting tayles, flying fish, & c.»

Many of those fish bear the same names today.

Further describing what substituted for manna in this hospitable and beautiful wilderness, Strachey wrote: «But above all these, most deservinge of observation are two sortes of birdes, the one (from the tune of his voice), the other (from the effect), called the cahowe and the egg bird, the latter arriving constantly on May 1, falls a layinge infinite stores of egges, upon certaine small sandy islands and so continue all that monthe, being all the while so tame and fearelesse that they suffer themselves to be thrust off their eggs: so that many thousands of egges (being as bigge as hens' egges) were eaten. The cahowe (for so sounded his voice) all the summer we saw not, and in the darkest nights of November and December (for in the night they onely feed) they would come forth, but not flye farre, making a strange hollow and harsh howling. These birds for their blindness (for they see weakly in the day) and for their cry, wee called the sea owle — wee caught them with a light bough in a darke night. Our men found a prettie way to take them which was by hollowing and laughing, with the noise thereof, the birds would come flocking and settle upon the very arms of him that so cryed: by which our men would weigh them and which weighed the heaviest they tooke, twentie dozen in two hours.»

As if fish and eggs were not sufficient, «There were wilde hogges upon the island. Our people would go a hunting with our ship dogge, and sometimes bring home thirtie boares, sowes and pigs in a weeke alive. From August and November they were well fed with berries that dropped from the cedars and palm but in February when the palm berries were scant and the cedar berries had failed two monthes sooner, true it is the hogges grew poore.»

It is speculated that these hogs were descendants of a cargo of hogs that were being carried to Cuba by Juan de Bermúdez more than a century before when he was wrecked on the islands to which he gave his name.

When the hogs grew poor, «then the tortoyses came in. Their meat is such as a man can neither absolutely call fish nor flesh, keeping most in the water and feeding upon sea-grasse like a heifer.»

They roasted the heart of the sabal palms, called cabbage palms in Florida, and used the leaves to thatch their cabins. It wasn't unalloyed bliss, though, for they did find prickle pears and poison ivy, which caused redness, itching, and blisters. There was no venomous creature on the Bermudas, and no human living there.

Those men, women, and children who had been going out to colonize Virginia set to work, under the direction of Admiral Somers, not only to keep alive but also to build ships, and they started a great tradition of ship-building on Bermuda. They put up rough shelters thatched with palm fronds. They mapped the string of islands, shaped like a fish-hook. A long boat was built and set sail to find aid for the marooned group. It was never seen again. Two other ships were built. A couple was wed, a man was killed, children were born during the nine months before the group finally sailed for Jamestown. What they found there was not nearly as good as what they had left in Bermuda, for famine and Indians had reduced the Jamestown colony to sixty people. They went back to Bermuda to get more food, and there Admiral Sir George Somers, a hardworking and able man, died on November 8, 1610. The island on which he died is called St. George's.

The First Permanent Settlement

The group sailed for England, leaving on Bermuda only three renegades. Thrilled by the tales the survivors brought home, the Virginia Company obtained the grant of the Bermudas from James I and in 1612 sent out the first permanent settlers, sixty people with ship's

Portrait of Sir George Somers by Van Somer

carpenter Richard Moore as governor. This was eight years before the Pilgrims landed at Plymouth Rock. Governor Moore inspired the colonists to build wharves for shipping and small forts to defend the islands against possible Spanish raids. They planted tobacco, corn, wheat, beans, and melons. A treasure of ambergris found on the shore was sent to England.

The colony was declining in energy when Bermuda was taken over by the Somers' Island Company under a new charter in 1615, and energetic Daniel Tucker was sent out as governor with new settlers. He is immortalized in a Mother Goose rhyme:

«Ole Dan Tucker was a funny old man,
He washed his face in a frying pan,
He combed his hair with a wagon wheel
And died with a toothache in his heel.»

His successor, Governor Nathaniel Butler, introduced parliamentary government to Bermuda, and the first General Assembly, which made local laws, was held on August 1, 1620. Bermuda's Parliament is the oldest in the British Commonwealth.

In the 1620s, spurred by Governor Butler, bridges were built between the main islands. Also a fort, a church, and a Sessions House were erected at St. George's, the capital town. In the building of the Sessions House a mortar made of lime and turtle oil was used to bind the limestone walls. It still stands, the oldest building in Bermuda.

A specially fitted ship was sent out from England to catch whales, and whaling became for a long time an important item in the Bermudian economy.

At this time Bermuda got its first coins, to replace the bartering that had been the way of trade in the islands. The coins had a hog on one side, to honor the wild hogs that had fed the first shipwrecked colonists, and the coins became known as «Hog Money.» They were of copper.

Slavery in Bermuda

The first slaves, one Indian and one Negro, were brought to Bermuda in 1616 to dive for pearls. Slavery soon came to be a way of life. Many more Negroes were brought from the West Indies, and some Indians from the English colonies in North America. Soon Bermuda had too many slaves. Because sugar cane, which needs much strong, cheap labor, was not so extensively grown in Bermuda as it was in the West Indies, there was not a real economic need for slavery. In the seventeenth and eighteenth centuries the majority of slaves were servants. There were several slave revolts on Bermuda, as in the other British colonies, and they were repressed with unspeakable cruelty. There were periods when the only fresh meat the slaves ever got was whale meat. There was «no manner of work to employ them advantageously. But the inhabitants have a pride in keeping of them,» reported one observer, describing slavery in Bermuda in the seventeenth century. He added, «No slaves in the West Indies are us'd so well as the Negroes are here.» The Negroes made good and trustworthy crewmen on the wide-ranging Bermuda sailing ships. In many instances in Bermuda there was much mutual dependence and affection between whites and their black servants. Many of the Negroes became skilled in the building trades.

More and more, in England, men were denouncing slavery as vile. The beginning of the end came in England when in 1772 Lord Chief

Justice Mansfield declared slavery to be «so odious that nothing could be suffered to support it but positive law.» Since that positive law did not exist in England, slavery became illegal there after that decision, and 14,000 colored people gained their freedom.

What was acclaimed as «one of the greatest events in the history of mankind» came on July 31, 1834, when all slaves in British colonies were set free. Though the English Abolition Law provided for a six year period of apprenticeship before complete freedom came, on Bermuda and Antigua all slaves were freed completely on August 1, 1834. Bermuda slave-owners received 128,340 pounds sterling in compensation.

Witchcraft and Superstitions

The witchcraft and superstitions of the West Indies are generally said to be African in origin. No such claim can be made as to the hysteria about witchcraft and the supernatural that prevailed in Bermuda for forty-six years, beginning with the arrival of Governor Josias Forster, who came in 1642 and encouraged the delusion. It came straight from England and northern Europe, which had been swept by this paranoid hysteria for years. King James I who commissioned the beautiful version of the Holy Bible that bears his name, believed thoroughly in witchcraft, wrote a book on the subject, and had laws passed providing hanging for witches. He has been called «the wisest fool in Christendom.»

Many Scottish prisoners who had fought for Charles I against Cromwell were sent to Bermuda in 1651 and sold as slaves. Scotland

16

was afire with the witch craze, and the Scots contaminated the Bermudians with their superstitions. Governor Forster began the dreadful era of witch trials.

It was held that a witch, who had made a pact with the Devil, could not drown because water would reject her. The test of a witch was to tie her hands and feet together and throw her in the water. If she floated, she was a witch. This was known as «swimming a witch.»

Old Jeanne Gardiner was so tested, and she floated and was hanged. She was the first of a series of men and women who were killed by neighbors' suspicions and talk. Witches and their male counterparts were accused of having the evil eye, of making psychic predictions and black magic, and of having a knowledge of magical herbs, potions, and poisons. It was not until the 1690s that this plague of the mind petered out, and the trials were discontinued. The witchcraft hysteria broke out in Salem, Massachusetts, in 1692.

Thereafter superstitions still prevailed in Bermuda, such as that a fabulous treasure was guarded by gnomes, that sudden squalls were raised by the devils. There is still belief in the supernatural and in the old folk-remedies, as there is just about everywhere. Some people in recent years have boasted of haunted houses and poltergeists.

The Bermuda Loyalists

When Oliver Cromwell led the Puritans to depose and behead King Charles I, Bermudians were predominantly Loyalist and protested bitterly. They elected a governor to declare Charles II their king. They sent the Puritans in Bermuda away, and some of those Bermudians became the first English settlers of the Bahamas under the leadership of William Sayle. Though he had been Governor of Bermuda three times, he went to England and formed «The Company of Eleutherian Adventurers» to take his fellow Puritans away to a new land. Claiming that the Puritans were persecuted in Bermuda, he founded a colony on the Bahama island he named Eleuthera.

As a result of all this, Cromwell's English Parliament declared in 1650 that Bermuda was in a state of rebellion and forbade any trade with the colony so long as the rebellion went on. The colony had to knuckle under and to acknowledge Cromwell's Commonwealth, but all Bermuda celebrated when Charles II became King of England in 1660.

Privateers and Pirates of Bermuda

Piracy and privateering began to flourish in the West Indies early in the sixteenth century. Attacks on the Spanish treasure fleets by bold spirits, first from France and then from Holland, began as early as the 1520s. The English soon joined them. Some of these pirate-privateers were highly respected, such as Sir John Hawkins and Sir Francis Drake. Sir Francis Drake declared that «an act of piracy against that cursed papist [The King of Spain] is an act of piety, so help us God.» And Queen Elizabeth II addressed Sir Francis, scourge of the Spanish, as «my dear pyrate.» Small tenant farmers and younger sons, as well as noble adventurers, were attracted to free-booting.

About the time Bermuda was being founded, piracy was flourishing not only in the Caribbean, but also in the North Sea, the English Channel, and the Mediterranean. Idleness was the background of much piracy, it is reported, and Ireland was the home of many pirates. Spain realized the importance of Bermuda as a bastion for pirates as soon as news reached Spain of colonizing by the English, but the small Spanish expedition sent against the young colony in 1614 backed off when fired upon.

Bermuda seafarers were turning to piracy, «because their fingers itched», within two decades of the founding of the colony. Bermuda officials also, early in the islands' history, were doing business with pirates. Ships commissioned in England to take pirates became pirates, which was the story of Captain William Kidd. During the seventeenth century it was still considered patriotic for Englishmen to attack and capture Spanish ships on the high seas.

Bermudians, who so often lacked supplies, welcomed any tramp ship of the sea that was not unfriendly. In the early years of the islands' history the company controlling the islands actually feared that revolt to the pirates by the people would take place, because of company mismanagement. By the middle of the seventeenth century, English and Dutch pirates infested Bermuda waters. Because the interests of the company were not identical with those of the colonists, and because the colonists were crippled by trade restrictions and administrative policies, the Bermudians were not reluctant to deal with pirates who did not harm them, and many of the islands' officials were rather openly corrupt.

The real license for respectable piracy by British seamen came in the eighteenth century and began with the War of Jenkins' Ear in 1739. Respectable sea banditry was called privateering. For almost a century after that time, privateering was big business in Bermuda. The period began with a treaty between England and Spain whereby England had the privilege of sending supplies in one ship each year either to Cartagena or Portobello in the Spanish West Indies. English merchants, being what they were in that era, began to send two ships, sometimes to both cities. One ship would land and discharge her cargo. At night, the ship would again be loaded with supplies from the second merchantman, standing offshore out of sight. The Spanish frequently showed their resentment at the violation of the treaty by attacking the illegal number two ship. One that they so attacked belonged to a sea captain called Jenkins, and he said the Spanish took not only his ship but his ear.

Jenkins showed his pickled ear round London and elicited such sympathetic rage that the populace wanted war. English officialdom said that Jenkins lost his ear for one of those crimes that had sent him to English prisons several times. The people prevailed, and England went to war against Spain. For about seventy-five years thereafter, England continued a series of almost unbroken wars with her European neighbors and, finally, toward the end of the period, with her American colonies.

Wealthy merchantmen of Bermuda promptly responded to the situation by fitting out privateers. The privateer captain had to have letters of marque to authorize him to attack enemy ships. There were a number of regulations governing the business, including the requirement that the privateer owner bring back his prize ship to an admiralty court, so that the court could make a judgment as to the legality of its seizure and as to the awards, based upon the value of the ship's cargo. Some of the swiftest ships ever built in Bermuda went to sea as privateers.

This is the way a privateersman was described in the eighteenth century: «Your true privateersman is a sort of half-horse, half-alligator, with a streak of lightning in his composition — something like a man-of-war's man, but much more like a pirate, with a superabundance of whisker, as if he held with Samson that his strength was in the quantity of his hair.» Privateersmen, it is reported, were nowhere well-disciplined and on shore were frequently disorderly.

Commissioning privateers who raided enemy shipping for profit obviously made good sense to England; they were the guerrilla troops of the ocean. But they finagled around, evaded regulations as to disposal of their cargoes, carried two sets of papers, and flouted the laws regulating privateering in all sorts of ways, including bribery of admiralty courts in Bermuda. They were not supposed to broach their cargo before it was adjudicated by an admiralty court, but this was a common practice. Many a privateersman was accused of attacking friendly shipping under false colors. The business thrived in the American Revolution and in the Napoleonic Wars, when French shipping was the enemy. The stakes were high — death or wealth. But there was no risk of life or limb to the Bermuda merchants who backed these seafaring ventures and reaped fortunes.

The lawless era came to an end in 1815, when peace treaties were made between England and the United States. While it lasted, it was a rough, jolly time.

TURK'S ISLAND

Adventurous Bermuda seafarers, in the hard years of the latter half of the seventeenth century, decided to found a colony of their own. In

1668 they sailed south almost a thousand miles, to a small island of rocks and glistening sand. Here they came ashore and found no inhabitants. They called it Turk's Island, because they found there a cactus that looked like the head of a man wearing a fez.

On Turk's Island they built huge salt ponds and raked salt during the hot months from May to October. This hard, hot work was the mainstay of the Bermuda economy for more than a century, for salt was a valued article of trade.

Life on Bermuda was full of welcomes and good-bys for many families for a long, long time indeed. Bermudians on Turk's Island were carried off as prisoners by the French in 1763. In 1801, though the Bermudians protested bitterly, Turk's Island and its salt industry were made part of the Bahama colony.

Bermuda Becomes a Crown Colony

Toward the end of the seventeenth century so many restrictions were enforced by the private investors who ruled the colony that the economy of the islands was being crippled. The colonists petitioned the Crown and sued the company, and the company forfeited its charter in 1684. The economy picked up. The Bermudians built ships of the fragrant cedar and traded in salt and food with the West Indies and America. Some became successful privateers during England's seemingly endless wars with France and Spain.

Bermuda's Seafarers and Their Sloops

This is how Sir Robert Robinson, who became Governor in 1687, described Bermuda in his day: «The people are of quick growth and well look't English countenance, but of a browner complexion, tall, lean, strong-limb'd and well-proportion'd. They are very frugal in their apparel, eating, drinking, and house furniture. Their houses are very neat and clean, usually of wood but an increasing number of stone.»

He wrote that the men are «hardy and generally good sailors... The women are likewise of large growth and are skilful in swimming and pilotting. They are commonly good housewives and are very amorous. They are generally handsome and courtly, love their husbands, their children and their dress. The children are chiefly exercised in fishing, swimming, diving and digging, and not in education which their parents do not cover nor does the island easily afford.» There were said to be three women to one man on the islands, since so many men lost their lives in shipwrecks.

It is easy to see why from the beginning Bermudians won wide fame as seafarers and boatbuilders. They had the deep, blue ocean all round them, their English heritage – and the great red cedar. Bermuda sloops came to be acclaimed as the best in the world for swiftness and long life. Many Bermuda ships were taken by pirates or privateers in the seventeenth and eighteenth centuries, but it is more than probable that Bermudians gained more through their privateering than they lost to pirates.

During the seventeenth century, Bermuda onions became a considerable item in export. In 1719, straw hats made of plaited Bermuda palmetto came into vogue among London ladies, and the palmetto «straw» was important in the export trade for some time. The soft limestone of the islands was cut into blocks, used as ballast, and traded as a building material in the West Indies and the Bahamas. It came into use as a versatile building material on the islands. It can be cut with a handsaw when it is first dug, and hardens when exposed to air. Blocks of the stone were used to make walls of buildings, and thin tiles were cut from it to roof the houses. The tiles are very porous when first cut, but when white-washed with lime and exposed to the air for some time they cannot be penetrated by water.

The Eighteenth Century

The eighteenth century opened with years of great hardship and a series of governors with whom the people feuded and bickered. Governor Samuel Day was called a tyrant, and it was said he clipped the edges of the coins to enrich himself. Governor Henry Pullein was a privateer and a rogue. Governor John Hope was, on the other hand, gallant and admired by the Bermudians.

(continued on page 55)

Approaching Bermuda from East

Approaching Bermuda from West →

← *Hamilton Harbour*

*Perot
Post Office
and Public
Library,
Hamilton*

*Par-la-Ville
Gardens*

← *Paget along
Harbour Road*

29

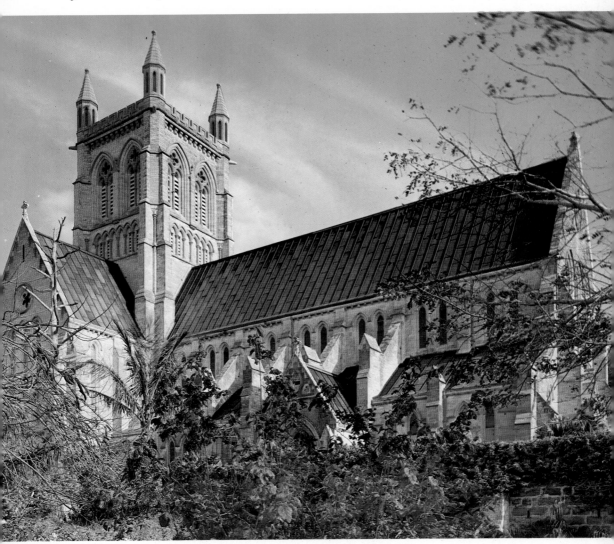

The Bermuda Cathedral (Anglican)

← *The Government House (Pembroke)*

St. Theresa's R. C. Cathedral, Hamilton

Paget with Salt Kettle

City Hall of Hamilton

Air View of Hamilton

The Princess Hotel
(Pembroke)

Botanical Gardens (Paget)

36

For detailed description see page 51

The Famous Beach, Elbow Beach Hotel (Paget)

Belmont Golf Club (Warwick)

Horseshoe Bay (Southampton) ↱

The Passion Flower

Cat's Claw-Vine

Bermudiana

BERMUDA

Mesembryanthemum

The Old Christ Church (Warwick)

For detailed description see page 52

Sonesta-Beach Hotel (Southampton)

A Sailboat Race

*Teddy Tucker, Famous Treasure Diver,
with Part of his Treasure*

For detailed description see page 53

*Teddy Tucker's Famous
Gold and Emerald Cross*

44

*Diving in the Clear Waters
of Bermuda*

Ely's Harbour

Mermaid Beach (Warwick)

The Royal Naval Dockyard

For detailed description see pages 53-54

Somerset Bridge,
World's Shortest Drawbridge

47

Description of foregoing pictures

Page 25
APPROACHING BERMUDA
The island group of Bermuda is clearly visible here from one end to the other, its picturesque shoreline broken by coves and sounds. The photograph shows the approach from the east in the late afternoon, with St. George's and St. David's Islands in the foreground. The second picture, page 27, taken from a lower angle, shows the beautiful colors of the clear ocean around Bermuda.

Pages 26 and 27
HAMILTON HARBOUR
This far extending safe harbor is a meeting place for elegant cruise ships of many countries. It is the heart of Hamilton, capital of Bermuda. Government buildings, banks, hotels and some of the most elegant stores are situated on Front Street, following the outline of the harbor.

← *Mangrove Bay
from Cambridge Beaches (Sandys)*

Page 28
PAGET, ALONG HARBOUR ROAD
A view over Hamilton Harbour to the attractive residential section of the Parish of Paget shows its many houses surrounded by gardens.

Page 29
PEROT POST OFFICE AND PUBLIC LIBRARY, HAMILTON
This is a view from Par-la-Ville Gardens in the back of two historical buildings. To the left is Par-la-Ville on Queen Street, now the home of the Public Library and the Bermuda Historical Society Museum. To the right is Perot Post Office of philatelic fame. Here postmaster William B. Perot issued Bermuda's first postage stamps by writing his signature across the Hamilton postmark. Par-la-Ville was his home.

PAR-LA-VILLE GARDENS
A beautiful city garden in the heart of Hamilton between Queen Street and Par-la-Ville Road, it is a favorite meeting place, especially at the lunch hour. This photograph shows the fine collection of trees and flowers typical of Bermuda.

Page 30

ON BUSY FRONT STREET, HAMILTON

Front Street, beside the Harbour of Hamilton, is one of the main streets of the capital city. The policeman who directs traffic on the busy corner of Queen and Front Streets is called «The Bobby in the Cage.»

Page 31

THE BERMUDA CATHEDRAL (Anglican)

On top of Church Hill overlooking Hamilton stands the Bermuda Cathedral, an impressive building in Middle English-Gothic style. Nearby is the residence of the Lord Bishop of Bermuda.

Page 32

GOVERNMENT HOUSE (Pembroke)

Residence of the governors of Bermuda since 1892, Government House on top of Mt. Langton Hill has a commanding view of the city of Hamilton. As one comes up the road to the main entrance, it looks like a stately castle surrounded by beautiful gardens planted with tropical, subtropical, and northern trees, shrubs, and plants. Up to 1814, the governor lived at St. George's, and in that year he moved to a residence on Mt. Langton Hill. In 1882 the Legislature authorized the erection of the new Government House, shown in this picture.

Page 33

ST. THERESA'S CHURCH, THE ROMAN CATHOLIC CATHEDRAL

Between the Academy of Mount St. Agnes Gardens and Victoria Park stands St. Theresa Church, a modern building with its entrance on Burnaby Street, Hamilton. It became the Roman Catholic Cathedral a short time ago.

PAGET WITH SALT KETTLE

A bird's-eye view from Great Sound over Hinson Island to Paget shows the Inverurie Hotel to the right and Salt Kettle in the center. The picture was taken after an ocean race, and the yachts are resting in safe water.

Page 34
THE CITY HALL
OF HAMILTON

Modern, but fitting appropriately into the picture of Hamilton, the fine City Hall was completed in 1960. Its ninety-one-foot tower is a landmark of Hamilton. The building contains galleries of the Bermuda National Gallery and the Bermuda Society of Arts, and a theater. It is a civic center for the entire island group.

Page 34
THE PRINCESS HOTEL
(Pembroke)

This beautiful modern hotel with its commanding location on Hamilton Harbour has a history, because it includes, in its present complex, parts of the old Princess Hotel, built in 1885. Every celebrity coming to the island stayed or visited there in the last decade of the nineteenth century.

Page 35
AERIAL VIEW OF HAMILTON

The photograph, taken above Paget and looking over Hamilton Harbour, shows the city and much of Pembroke Parish.

Page 36
BOTANICAL GARDENS

Known also as the Bermuda Public Garden, the Botanical Gardens are situated in eastern Paget, within the Agricultural Station on South and Berry Hill Roads. These are magnificent gardens, with a wide variety of Bermuda flowers.

Page 37
ELBOW BEACH HOTEL
(Paget)

One of the great hotels on the South Shore of Bermuda, in Paget, is the Elbow Beach Hotel. Its big pool overlooks a magnificent private beach on the tranquil, leeward side of the island.

BELMONT GOLF CLUB (Warwick)

Bermuda is a paradise for golfers. Many of the great golf courses of the world are found here, and one of them is the Belmont Golf Club, surrounding the Belmont Hotel. It is an eighteen-hole, par-68 course with beautiful views over the Great Sound.

Pages 38-39
HORSESHOE BAY (Southampton)

The most beautiful public beach of Bermuda is undoubtedly at Horseshoe Bay. Stretching for about half a mile along the South Shore, it has the finest of white-sand beaches, framed by dramatic rock formations that shelter sun-bathers from the wind.

Pages 40-41
FLOWERS OF BERMUDA: THE PASSION FLOWER

This exotic flower, grown commercially in Bermuda, is a favorite for corsages and flower arrangements. The vine on which it grows thrives in the islands.

BERMUDIANA

A native of the islands, this lovely blue flower blooms profusely from March to May, especially along the beaches. It is the national flower of Bermuda.

CAT'S-CLAW VINE

Typical of Bermuda is this yellow flower of the vine that grows on old walls all over the islands.

MESEMBRYANTHEMUM

This subtropical succulent plant with its trailing habit of growth blooms luxuriantly in Bermuda.

Page 42
THE OLD CHRIST CHURCH (Church of Scotland), WARWICK

This church, built in 1719, is the oldest Presbyterian church in the western hemisphere. Adjoining is Thorburn Memorial Hall, erected in memory of Reverend Walter Thorburn, minister of the church from 1852 to 1882.

Page 43
SONESTA BEACH HOTEL

With its unusual location on a rock formation surrounded by a splendid beach of the South Shore of Southampton, the Sonesta Beach Hotel is one of the best and newest hotels in Bermuda.

A SAILBOAT RACE

Races are a favorite sport in Bermuda on weekends and on special occasions.

Page 44
TEDDY TUCKER WITH PART OF HIS TREASURE

Bermuda-born Teddy Tucker is an internationally famous treasure diver who has salvaged treasures worth millions of dollars from sunken ships in waters around Bermuda. He was born in 1925 in Paget, son of Edward Henry Tucker, a marine surveyor and architect. He served as a diver in the Royal Navy during World War II. He lives with wife, Edna, in Somerset, Bermuda.

TEDDY TUCKER'S FAMOUS GOLD AND EMERALD CROSS

In an astonishing outrage this sixteenth-century gold and emerald cross was stolen just before it was to be shown to Queen Elizabeth II at the opening of the Bermuda Maritime Museum in 1975.

Page 45
DIVING IN THE CLEAR WATERS OF BERMUDA

Bermuda is the most northern island group around which corals now grow. Brain coral, gorgonians, and softly waving sea-fans, surrounded by colorful fish, make a vivid impression on the reef diver. The picture shows gorgonians to the right and brain coral in the center.

ELY'S HARBOUR

Bermuda's most western bay is Ely's Harbour, a sheltered stretch of water that is perfect for small-craft sailing, water skiing, and other aquatic sports.

Page 46
MERMAID BEACH

Here is another romantic beach, surrounded by picturesque rock formations. It is part of a cottage colony of the same name on the South Shore of Warwick.

Page 47
THE ROYAL NAVY DOCKYARD ON IRELAND ISLAND

This was once a key British naval base and today houses Bermuda's

Maritime Museum. A series of exhibitions are staged here which chronicle Bermuda's association with the Royal Navy and long maritime history.

SOMERSET BRIDGE, WORLD'S SHORTEST DRAWBRIDGE

Said to be the shortest drawbridge in the world, Somerset Bridge connects Southampton with Somerset Island in Sandys Parish.

Page 48
MANGROVE BAY FROM CAMBRIDGE BEACHES

At the northwest end of Bermuda on Sandys coast is Mangrove Bay, with some of the most romantic scenery in the islands. The picture shows a view to the southeast over the Bay, with Somerset Village in the background.

Hamilton Harbour, circa 1868

(continued from page 24)

Bermuda and the American Revolution

The news of the shots fired at Bunker Hill was received, when it finally reached Bermuda on its way around the world, with consternation. The majority of the islanders were Loyalists, though a number of prominent families sympathized with the American colonists. War between England and her American colonies meant that Bermuda's food supply would be cut off and trade would be ruined.

The American colonists desperately needed gunpowder, while Bermudians sent delegates to the Continental Congress in Philadelphia in 1775 to beg for food. General George Washington promptly wrote to the inhabitants of the islands, asking for their sympathy. He said that he was informed that there was a very large powder magazine on Bermuda with a feeble guard, and asked tactfully if the American colonists might avail themselves of this supply. On a dark night in 1775 a band of quiet and speedy men broke into the powder magazine on Bermuda and rolled one hundred barrels of gunpowder down the hill through the back park of the staunchly Loyalist governor. They were loaded into whale-boats waiting along the shore and taken to sloops ready to sail. Rewards were posted for information leading to the conviction of the culprits, but they were never apprehended.

As a result, the Continental Congress authorized the shipment of a year's provisions to Bermuda. Bermudians also sailed from Turk's Island with salt for the Americans, who needed that commodity. As the war went on, the famished islanders on Bermuda became more and more dependent on American corn. Britain then sent victuals. In the end,

Bermuda largely remained loyal to the Crown. Bermuda privateers raided American shipping, and Bermuda's ships were captured and invasion was threatened by the American revolutionaries. Many Loyalists from the thirteen American colonies came to the islands.

Nowhere was peace more welcome than on Bermuda. Trading resumed and times got better. The **Bermuda Gazette,** the first newspaper, was started in 1784.

HAMILTON

Smith's Island was the first seat of government. Soon the government was moved to St. George's Towne. As a capital, St. George's Towne, on the eastern end of the island chain, was not ideally situated. A central location would be much more convenient. Governors began to try to change the capital to a more central location early in the eighteenth century. The problem was, as one writer noted in that era, «for the last forty years each individual has been aiming at a Towne within a hundred yards of his nativity.»

Construction of the town of Hamilton began in 1792 with the backing of Governor Henry Hamilton, after whom it is named. The capital was moved in 1815 during Admiral Cockburn's administration.

A custom house warehouse was built, and four forts to defend the islands against the French. A coffee house and stores soon followed. Merchants began to grow wealthy through their ownership of shares in privateering vessels operating in the West Indies. A visiting acrobat performed in Hamilton in 1796. As the years went swiftly by, schools and churches were built, fire and fever occasionally hit, and the sea which dominates Bermuda shaped the life of the delightful town rising on the rolling hills above the harbor. Hamilton has never been a dull town, having always been prone to balls, quadrilles, band concerts, and flirtations.

Tom Moore in Bermuda

Tom Moore, the Irish poet, strolled the streets and lanes of Bermuda but briefly, but the memory of his curls and charm and of his lyrics is still fresh in the islands, and his was Bermuda's most celebrated flirtation. He was what all Irishmen want to be—handsome, a poet, and a great social success. He came young out of Ireland to London, floating on the crest of the popularity of his first lyrics. His social success in London proved so expensive that he was glad, with the help of a princely patron, to go to Bermuda in 1803 as registrar of the admiralty prize courts in the islands.

He did not make the money he had been led to believe would be his, and so he stayed only three months. But while there he flirted, was wined and dined, and stored memories that led him to write most fondly of those islands and of a lady who lived there. His charm caused him to be most hospitably received, and it is of this hospitality, in part, that he later sang. To a young matron seven months married, he wrote the verses of «Nea.».

That she was indeed a Bermudian, the scenery of the verse attests:

> «Behold the leafy mangrove, bending
> O'er the waters blue and bright,
> Like Nea's silky lashes, lending
> Shadow to her eyes of light!»

His «Ode to the Calabash Tree» is still so well remembered that «Moore's calabash tree,» under which he sat, is pointed out today, dense and luxuriant with age. The golden sands, the tint of bowers, the cottages «white as the palace of a Lapland gnome» — Moore wrote about them all. The flavor, the fragrance, and the beauty of Bermuda were recalled by Tom Moore long after his three months' stay in the islands. Nine years later he wrote:

> «Oh, had we some bright little isle of our own,
> In a blue summer ocean far off and alone...
> Where simply to feel that we breathe, that we live
> Is worth the best joy that life elsewhere can give.»

He was not the first nor the last to feel the magic of Bermuda, but he captured it so deftly in his lyrics that he is still well enshrined in island legends.

Moore appointed a deputy in Bermuda and returned to London, where he wrote successful poems, lyrics for songs, satires, and political squibs. The deputy he left in Bermuda embezzled a large sum, for which Moore was liable, and Moore had to go live on the Continent to avoid debtors' prison until he negotiated a settlement of the Bermuda affair. This does not seem to have soured his memories of the islands.

THE NAPOLEONIC WARS

After a brief period of brisk trade between Bermuda and the rest of the world following the end of the American Revolution, war between England and France heated up. If there had been mixed emotions in Bermuda regarding the American Revolution, there were none in the Napoleonic Wars or in the War of 1812-1815 between England and the United States. Bermudians were totally loyal to England. French privateers raided Bermuda shipping, and Bermuda privateers excelled all others. Admiral Nelson, who had served in the West Indies, finally sank Napoleon's dream by sending the French fleet to the bottom at the Battle of Trafalgar Bay in 1805, where Nelson won immortality and lost his life. For the fastest way to get the news of the victory and the loss to England, the English sent it in a Bermuda sloop, the **Pickle.**

It was from Bermuda, through the North Rock passage, that the British fleet took off in 1814 to attack the capital of the United States. With 3,500 troops aboard and a good passage to the Chesapeake, this fleet attacked and burned Washington.

THE DOCKYARD

It became so obvious that Bermuda might become the Gibraltar of the West if properly fortified that in 1810 Britain began to build a dockyard and a naval station on Ireland Island. Work began with local labor and British funds. The movement to build a mighty fortress there

59

began in the American Revolution and resulted finally in Bermuda's becoming the headquarters of the America and West Indies Squadron of the Royal Navy. To assist in the work on the dockyard, convicts were sent out from England for forty years. More than 9,000 men were sent to Bermuda from England in that period, and old ships were used for their prisons. They not only worked on the dockyard, they cut roads into the limestone. The Imperial Dockyard on the West End was a tremendous boon to the islands' economy in the nineteenth century, and not until 1951 was it closed.

The Bermuda Clippers

The first steamship came into Hamilton Harbour in 1833, amazing those seafaring islanders. But the greatest days of the sailing ships were yet to come. Those great white birds of the nineteenth century, that could move across the water faster than the early steamships, became known as Yankee clippers. They originated, however, in Baltimore, where the first big clipper was built in 1833. The Bermuda shipbuilders contributed their share to the beauty that followed, spurred by the competition of the new steamships.

Some of the fastest and most graceful ships that ever sailed were the clipper barques built on Bermuda during the 1850s and 1860s. They were long, slender vessels with a long, sharp, bow. They carried three rakish masts, and the square-rigged sails were crowded on. Veteran seamen said at the time they were launched that they were the most beautiful things ever built in Bermuda. They sailed for decades between

The Koh-I-Noor, handsomest of Bermuda's clipper barques, launched 1855

Bermuda and New York, the West Indies and Britain. They beat steamships. The five fast Bermuda clippers built in Bermuda between 1853 and 1864 were the **Sir George F. Seymour,** the **Koh-I-Noor,** the **Pearl,** the **Cedric** and the **Lady Milne.**

The clippers carried arrowroot, onions, potatoes, tomatoes, passengers, and convicts going home to Ireland from Bermuda, and they returned with supplies to the island. Arrowroot, from which a fine starch is made, was a staple of the island trade at that time. Whales were still taken along the coast, furnishing not only oil but «sea beef.» When William Reid came out in 1839 to serve as governor, he found only two ploughs in Bermuda. He imported more ploughs and held ploughing contests, and the export of arrowroot increased. The first lighthouse was built during his term as governor, and the whale-oil light went on in 1846 on Gibb's Hill. He also founded a public library in 1839, the first on Bermuda.

The Civil War in the United States

To Bermuda, as to the Bahamas, the Civil War in the United States from 1861 to 1865 brought a great tide of prosperity. The sympathy of the majority of Bermudians was with the South, for many had families or trade relations in Virginia, North Carolina, and South Carolina. Since Bermuda men excelled on the sea, they proved to be great blockade runners. England, with mills that needed cotton, shipped arms, ammunition, and other badly needed supplies to the South through Bermuda. It was a rewarding if highly dangerous test of skill in the fast, shallow-draft Bermuda sloops to evade the Northern ships blockading Southern ports. St. George's and Hamilton Harbour were thronged with ships, and their warehouses and wharves were crammed with goods going and coming.

Though Queen Victoria had forbidden her subjects to get involved in that war, few doubted the South would win, and the blockade-runners were heroes in Bermuda. Many ships were seized or sunk. Many more made fortunes. The United States Navy attempted to blockade St. George's Harbour but desisted after sharp protests by British authorities.

An economic slump followed the American Civil War, and the building up of Bermuda as a major British fortress of the Atlantic again helped to save the colony from an economic downturn.

Trouble threatened with Venezuela. Victorian land forces were stationed in Bermuda, and barracks were built for them near the naval forts at the dockyard. Nine large forts were repaired or built. The largest floating dock, the most modern facility to serve ships of its time, was towed across the Atlantic to Bermuda in 1869. The thirty-six-day trip was an uneventful success, to the delight and wonder of the islanders.

THE PORTUGUESE

To take up the slack in the economy after the Civil War, the Bermudians also concentrated on agriculture and on increasing their exports. The population concentrated on growing potatoes, onions, and tomatoes for export in the chilly season when vegetables could not be grown in North America. With the increase in vegetable farming and export, Portuguese farmers came in from the Azores. They were the migrant workers of their day. They were welcomed, and many stayed to live in Bermuda. More Portuguese were brought in from the Azores in 1923-1924, when the same farm labor was needed. Today there are several thousand Bermudians of Portuguese descent, characterized by thrift and energy.

Seeds of the Tourist Industry

Before there was a United States of America, Bermuda had achieved a reputation as a delightful place to visit because of its healthful climate. In 1779 Maryland showed her goodwill to the many islanders who were helping the American Revolutionaries by granting to one of her prominent citizens the right to go past the wartime embargo to visit Bermuda for his health. It was widely known even then for its fine climate for invalids.

With the renewed endeavor to raise and export vegetables to the United States and Canada during the last half of the nineteenth century, the ships that carried the freight away from the islands began also to carry passengers. They were not the modern, luxurious cruise ships of today. Mark Twain said, «Bermuda is a paradise... but one must go through hell to get there.» William Dean Howells, Mark Twain's friend, wrote in 1885 of Bermuda's capital, Hamilton, «I should think it a rich enough experience to spend my whole time lounging up and down the

The Princess Hotel, 1885

sloping streets.» Princess Louise, daughter of Queen Victoria and wife of the governor general of Canada, visited Bermuda in 1882. The princess conquered hearts and was conquered by the charms of the islands. She drove about in a little phaeton and sailed about in a skiff.

Promptly, a second hotel called The Princess was built in Hamilton in her honor. A new bank was founded. Three large schools which still serve Bermuda were founded between 1888 and 1893, Saltus Grammar School, Mount St. Agnes Academy, and Bermuda High School for Girls. Tourists began to come in sufficient numbers to keep two hotels open all year, and before long there were other hotels open only in the winter.

The reputation of Bermuda grew, and more and more visitors came to relax, get warm in the winter, and restore their souls with beauty. The island became one of the first winter resorts for North America and probably inspired Henry Flagler's Palm Beach. A new lighthouse, St. David's Lighthouse, began to shine in 1879. A regatta had been organized for Princess Louise, and in 1882 the first organized Bermuda dinghy races were sailed. Tennis was introduced into Bermuda from England in 1873, and from Bermuda into the United States. Telephones were introduced in 1887 and electric light in 1904. Sir Thomas Lipton put up a cup for the first of the Biennial Ocean Races, which was sailed in 1906. The islands had always been hospitable, from the time the shipwrecked English colonists headed for Jamestown came ashore in 1609. It dawned upon the Bermudians that hospitality to visitors could be an attractive industry and a pleasant way of life. Tourism, that great industry of the twentieth century, was born.

WORLD WAR I

War in 1914 again meant hardship to Bermuda, with shipping crippled and supplies limited. Bermuda fishermen could not go to the outermost banks for fear of being captured by German warships. Bermuda volunteers and militia were mobilized to guard the island fortress of the British Navy. Bermuda contingents served with the British Army in France.

PROHIBITION

No single event had such a stimulating and immediate effect on Bermuda's economic well-being as the passage of the Volstead Act in the United States. Tourists flocked in to drink decent whiskey in a uniquely beautiful little island resort. Luxury liners plied the sea between Bermuda and New York and kept the new hotels that were being built full of visitors. The Mid-Ocean Golf Course was created. Bermuda seafarers turned their talents to rum-running. The islands boomed.

The Suntan Revolution

In the 1920s a profound cultural change began to come about in the United States, and later it spread to some extent in England. It was to have a wide effect that still continues. Bermuda pioneered in contributing to the change. This change was in the attitude of well-to-do people toward being suntanned. For ages a fair complexion had been considered most elegant and desirable among people of English origin. The skin tones of blond ladies unkissed by the sun were what English poets praised. In the United States, and especially in the South, a «peaches-and-cream» complexion was prized as proof of the fact that the possessor thereof did not have to work in the fields in the sun. Sun bonnets had excellent sales. Then the rich and famous began in considerable numbers to go vacationing in Bermuda – sailing, golfing, swimming.

A suntan began to have prestige. It was proof positive in winter that anyone who sported a browned skin could afford to take the time off and to spend the money needed to go to sunny lands to play.

After a suntan became a status symbol, Bermuda's summer tourism received a big boost. The climate had always been pleasant in the summer, and the water more inviting for water sports than in the winter. A year-round tourist economy was born, and it continued to prosper in the 1930s even during Depression in the United States.

In spite of this profound sociological change, Bermuda did not give women the right to vote until 1944. It was not until the 1950s that South Florida resorts were able to achieve the stability that results from attracting summer sun-lovers in considerable numbers.

WORLD WAR II

The tourist economy went into hibernation in this war, but the economic effects were not so brutal as in other countries. German submarines became so menacing to North Atlantic shipping that Great Britain asked Bermuda to give land for the establishment of U.S. naval and military bases. One-tenth of the land of the islands was given on a ninety-nine-year lease, and shoal waters were also filled to build the bases. These became vital to the safety of the convoys of men and material that helped to defeat Hitler. From these islands the Royal Navy patrolled the Atlantic. The United States built an airfield that still serves Bermuda today.

THE SPACE RACE

The peacetime alliance between Bermuda and the United States was strengthened when in 1959 the U.S. National Aeronautics and Space Administration was given the right to build a tracking station for space vehicles on Cooper's Island. Bermuda has also been a major base for the exploration of «inner space,» the ocean. In 1964, Operation Sealab was carried out thirty miles southwest of Bermuda on the Argus Bank. This scientific experiment tested the ability of men to live deep underwater for ten days, and was followed by many other experiments.

The end of the cold war means that Britain and the United States have decided to give up their Bermuda bases, and, in 1994, it was expected they would revert to Bermuda in a few years' time.

BERMUDA TODAY

There is no problem in visiting Bermuda today, except most visitors must remember to drive on the lefthand side of the road. Frequent jet flights are scheduled to the islands from England, Canada, and the United States. There are also frequent cruise ships. Official identification (passport or certified birth certificate) of U.S. citizenship is required of U.S. citizens as well as a return or onward air ticket.

The local currency is on a par with the U.S. dollar, which is accepted everywhere. There are excellent overseas phone and cable services between Bermuda and the rest of the world. Transportation by taxi, bicycle, bus, moped, carriage and ferry is easy to obtain.

Complete facilities and equipment for just about every outdoor sport may be found here. They play cricket in Bermuda from May through September, and soccer from October through April. There are many tennis courts, including public courts at the Bermuda Tennis Stadium. Horseback riding is available. Spectator sports include horse racing and boxing.

In the water world, there are cruises to the Sea Gardens in glass-bottom boats. Sightseeing on the water is also done by catamaran and motor-yacht cruises. Sailboats, ranging from small Sunfish to larger yachts with a licensed skipper, are for hire. To explore the beautiful underwater world of the coral reefs there are snorkel tours, SCUBA diving tours, and helmet diving tours. Water skiing can be enjoyed both as a spectator sport and as a participating sport.

All sorts of night-time entertainment enliven the evenings, from motion pictures to exciting night clubs and lavish floor shows in some of the hotels. Free-port shopping, with luxurious articles from all over the world, makes Hamilton a shopper's paradise.

Some of the most modern and luxurious resort hotels, clubs, and cottage colonies in the world receive visitors to Bermuda. They range from casual, informal, and inexpensive to formal and quite expensive. Many private homes take guests.

Among the best places are these:

Large Resort Hotels: Belmont Hotel and Golf Club, Elbow Beach, Grotto Bay Beach, Harmony Club, Marriott's Castle Harbour Resort, Mermaid Beach, Palm Reef, Princess (Hamilton), Sonesta Beach, Southampton Princess, and Stonington Beach.

Small Hotels: Glencoe, Newstead, Palmetto Hotel and Cottages, Pompano Beach Club, The Reefs, Rosedon, Royal Palms Club, Waterloo House, and White Sands.

Clubs: Coral Beach and Tennis Club, and Mid Ocean Club.

Cottage Colonies: Ariel Sands, Cambridge Beaches, Horizons, Lantana, Pink Beach and Willowbank.

Guest Houses, and Large Housekeeping Cottages and Apartments: Angels Grotto Apartments, Barnsdale Guest Apartments, Brightside Guest Apartments, Cabana Vacation Apartments, Greenbank Guest House and Cottages, Hillcrest Guest House, Loughlands, Marley Beach, Mermaid West, Munro Beach, Pretty Penny, Rosemont, Royal Palms Club, Salt Kettle House, Sky-Top Cottages, South Capers, Surf Side Beach, White Heron, and Woodbourne/Inverness.

SEEING BERMUDA

If you can tear yourself away from the sun-splashed beaches or the confines of luxury hotels with which Bermuda is liberally sprinkled, you will discover that there is much to explore and to enjoy on virtually every one of Bermuda's 13,177 acres. In spite of its postage-stamp size, Bermuda offers much variety both in activity and scene. Sport of every kind may be enjoyed by the visitor and the landscape is rich in natural beauty. To roam the islands is to enjoy magnificent sea views, lovely beaches, hidden coves, and enchanting gardens along country lanes. You may board a variety of boats to cruise among the islands, visit the sea gardens or explore the reefs and wrecks below the sea.

HAMILTON

Hamilton has been the capital of Bermuda for almost 150 years, when, in spite of tremendous opposition from the east-enders, the seat of Government was transferred from St. George's in 1815. Tucked between a hillside and the sea within a space of 182 acres, Hamilton is the hub of the island's transportation services, a shopping center for choice merchandise and a colonial capital of considerable historic interest. Many of today's shops were the residences of Hamilton's first citizens.

Albouy's Point. Any tour of Hamilton should include Albouy's Point, the home of the Royal Bermuda Yacht Club, founded in 1844.

Par-la-Ville. A fine old house on Queen Street which is at present the home of the Public Library and Bermuda Historical Society Museum. This was formerly the home of William B. Perot, a Bermudian postmaster of the middle 19th century who put the colony on the philatelic map by writing his name across the Hamilton postmark and sold them as stamps, thereby creating a rare and most sought-after item. The Historical Society Museum contains a portrait of Sir George Somers and his lady, a good collection of Bermuda furniture, and interesting relics past and present. A hundred-year-old rubber tree grows in front of the house, and in the rear are the beautiful Par-la-Ville Gardens, which are among the loveliest in the colony. Next door is the recently restored Perot Post Office, home of the famous stamp.

(continued on page 104)

In the Harbor of St. George's

Air View of St. George's

St. Peter's Church, St. George's

For detailed description see page 97

Replica of the 17th-century ship Deliverance

Historical Jail Window →

Fort St. Catherine

Historical Society Museum

ST. GEORGE'S

Typical Bermuda Roof →

Joseph Stockdale House

The Annual Peppercorn Ceremony, St. George's

For detailed description see page 99

**BERMUDA
PAGEANTRY**

Noonday Cannon Salute, St. George's

Skirling Ceremony at Fort Hamilton

The Old Rectory, St. George's

For detailed description see pages 99-100

*The Old
Bridge House*

*HISTORICAL HOUSES
IN ST. GEORGE'S*

Confederate Museum

←Church Ruins, St. George's

Fishing is Good in Bermuda

Tucker's Town Bay

Easter Lilies at the Bermuda Perfumery

Castle Harbour Golf Club (First Hole) →

Marriott's Castle Harbour Hotel, Tucker's Town

PAR FOR THIS COURSE
IS 4 HOURS
A BIRDIE IS 3 HRS
AN EAGLE IS 2 HRS
NOW'S YOUR CHANCE
TO BE A PAR BUSTER

Castle Island Beach

Natural Arches,
Tucker's Town

Mid Ocean Golf Club, Tucker's Town

For detailed description see pages 101-102

Gene Steede, Noted Calypso Singer

Evening in Hamilton Harbour

← *Crystal Caves*

*Dancing
under the Stars*

Palm Grove Garden (Devonshire)

Rental Transportation

North Coast at the Crawl →

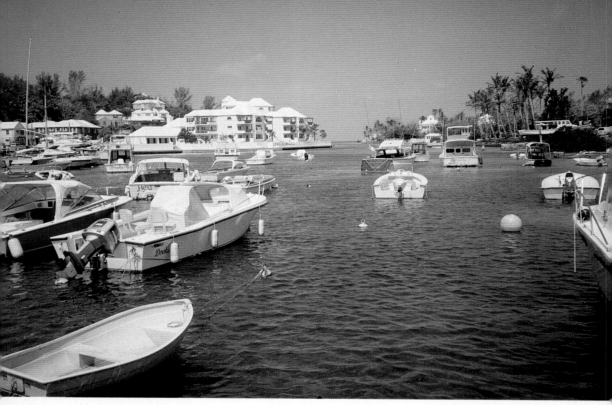

Flatts Inlet

For detailed description
see page 103

*Waterskiing is
very Popular in Bermuda*

Sunfish Regatta on Harrington Sound

Description of foregoing pictures

Page 73
IN THE HARBOR
OF ST. GEORGE'S

The harbor of the oldest English settlement still existing in the western hemisphere is small and colorful. The picture shows Ordnance Island, with St. George's Dinghy and Sports Club dominating the harbor.

Page 74
AERIAL VIEW OF ST. GEORGE'S

The picture shows the main streets which run parallel to the waterfront and, near the center of the photograph, King's Square with the Town Hall, which was erected in 1808. On the right is Ordnance Island, home to the replica of the Deliverance, and below that Somers Wharf.

Page 75
ST. PETER'S CHURCH,
ST. GEORGE'S

St. Peter's is the oldest Anglican church in continuous use in the New World. The first wooden church was built by the first governor, Richard Moore, in 1612, but a more substantial building was erected here in 1619. The church was rebuilt again in its present form in 1713 and enlarged in 1814. The cedar altar has been in use since 1624.

Page 76
17TH-CENTURY SHIP
DELIVERANCE

The Deliverance *and her consort, the* Patience, *were built by survivors of the* Sea Venture *and carried them safely to Jamestown ten months after the shipwreck. On the waterfront at St. George's, Ordnance Island, is a superb replica of the* Deliverance.

FORT ST. CATHERINE

St. George's is surrounded by forts. Gate's Fort, to the east, was built in 1612. To the north, construction began on Fort St. Catherine in 1613 and continued in the eighteenth and nineteenth centuries until 1880, when Bermuda had become the "Gibraltar of the West." Never was a shot fired in anger from this massive fortification. The fort is open to the public and displays replicas of the Crown Jewels of England. The beautiful beach in front is used by guests of the nearby Bermuda Beach Hotel. The lower photograph shows an air view of Fort St. Catherine.

Page 77
HISTORICAL JAIL WINDOW

Through this grated window from his cell in the old jail in St. George's, the Reverend John Stephenson, first Methodist missionary to Bermuda, preached to the people gathered outside. He cut in the cedar floor in his cell: «John Stephenson, Methodist Missionary, was imprisoned in this jail 6 months and fined 50 pounds for preaching the gospel of Jesus Christ to African Blacks and captive Negroes. St. George's, Bermuda, June 1801.»

Page 78
Historical Society Museum

Housed in a picturesque old house built in 1725 on Featherbed Alley, the museum shows how Bermudians lived in the early days. The hand-carved Bermuda cedar table in the living room was used 350 years ago in the old State House. There is a letter from General George Washington, dated in 1775, asking for gunpowder from Bermuda, and copies of the Royal Gazette *from 1784. (See also picture on page 81.)*

Joseph Stockdale House

Situated on Printer Alley, this was the house of Joseph Stockdale, who in 1783 brought the first printing press to Bermuda. He was the founder of the Royal Gazette, *Bermuda's first newspaper.*

Page 79
TYPICAL BERMUDA ROOF, ST. GEORGE'S

The roofs of most of the Bermuda houses are made of native limestone. They are constructed of inch-thick slates laid over a stone gutter at the angle appropriate for the purpose of leading every drop of rainwater into a water tank beneath the house. Each household is responsible for its own water supply. The picture shows the roof of an old Bermuda house, built in 1725, now the Historical Society Museum.

Page 80
THE PEPPERCORN CEREMONY, ST. GEORGE'S

When the government moved from St. George's to Hamilton in 1816, the State House was rented to Bermuda's oldest Masonic Lodge, St. George under the Scottish constitution charter dated August 7, 1797. The annual rental is one peppercorn. The payment of this rent has become the occasion for a most colorful ceremony. The date was formerly December 27, the Feast of St. John the Evangelist. Later it was changed to fall on the most convenient date nearest April 23, St. George's Day.

Page 81
BERMUDA PAGEANTRY

There are colorful ceremonies in winter especially. A highlight in

Hamilton is the «Skirling Ceremony,» held in Fort Hamilton. At noon, kilted pipers and drummers perform on the ramparts of the fort, which commands a breathtaking view of the city, the harbor, and the island.

From November to February, every Wednesday the mayor of St. George's personally greets visitors to the old town. Just before noon the Bermuda Regiment marches into the town square and, following a fanfare, the traditional noonday cannon salute is fired by a uniformed guard. There is also a colorful show of the Bermuda Regiment at Gate's Fort.

Page 82
THE OLD RECTORY, ST. GEORGE'S

This romantic house belonging to the National Trust is a gem of early Bermuda architecture. It was the home of George Dew, a pardoned pirate of the early 18th century, who became a respected citizen of St. George's. Midcentury it became the rectory, when the Reverend Alexander Richardson married the widowed lady whose home it was.

Page 83
THE OLD BRIDGE HOUSE

Just behind the Town Hall is the old Bridge House, so called because there was once a bridge here over a lagoon that divided the town. The lagoon was filled in to become Somers Garden. Bridge House was once a governor's residence. Edward Goodrich bought it in 1787 from his brother, Bridger. Both brothers owned several privateers during the French wars.

The Confederate Museum
on Duke of York Street was built by Governor Samuel Day in 1699 in the garden of the old Government House as his private residence. It was later converted into a hotel and was used during the American Civil War as the headquarters of the Confederate agents. It was the hub of high adventure in the days of blockade-running out of Bermuda.

Page 84
CHURCH RUINS, ST. GEORGE'S

This church on Duke of Kent Street was to have replaced St. Peter's, the historical Anglican parish church, which was badly in need of repair. The foundations of the new church, planned as a magnificent example of Victorian Gothic, were laid in 1874, but it was never finished. Money ran low, and interest in restoring St. Peter's revived. And so today flowers and bushes are the church's only congregation, and birds its choir.

Page 85
TUCKER'S TOWN BAY

Tucker's Town on the southeastern coast of Bermuda was founded in the hope that it would become the capital of Bermuda. With Castle Harbour as a perfect approach from the ocean, it would have been a fine location. But the capital was moved from St. George's to Hamilton. Today Tucker's Town is one of the most exclusive and elegant residential sections of Bermuda, with a fine white-sand beach on the South Shore, a safe harbor, and two of the best golf courses, Castle Harbour and Mid Ocean.

FISHING IS GOOD IN BERMUDA

Shore, reef, and deep-sea fishing are all great around Bermuda. There are plenty of bonefish, pompano, and gray snapper along the shore. Amberjack, yellowtail, chub, and rockfish live among the coral reefs. Blue and white marlin, blackfin tuna, Allison tuna, dolphin, wahoo, and bonito are caught in the deep waters surrounding the islands.

Page 86
EASTER LILIES AT THE BERMUDA PERFUMERY

Fields of blooming Easter lilies cover Bermuda in April and May. Brought from China in the nineteenth century to Bermuda, they grew so well there that they were soon being grown all over the islands. Flowers are exported to the United States and Canada.

MARRIOTT'S CASTLE HARBOUR HOTEL

The centers of social activity around Tucker's Town are the Mid Ocean Club and Marriott's Castle Harbour Hotel, one of the most elegant hotels of the islands, with two swimming pools, an eighteen-hole championship golf course, beautiful gardens, private beach, and tennis courts.

Page 87
CASTLE HARBOUR GOLF CLUB (First Hole)

The first hole at Castle Harbour is the most scenic opener of any on Bermuda's seven links. Looking down from the attractive new club house, the picture shows the beautiful view of the golf course with the brilliant blue-green waters of Castle Harbour to the left. In the background, deep blue, is the Atlantic Ocean. The eighteen-hole course has a total yardage of 6,142.

Page 88
CASTLE ISLAND BEACH

Far east on the Castle Roads connecting the ocean with Castle Harbour is Castle Island, known for its strong fortifications, the King's Castle, and the notorious Black Hole. Here also is a romantic beach, shown in the picture.

NATURAL ARCHES, TUCKER'S TOWN

The coast of Bermuda has many dramatic and unusual rock formations. The Natural Arches on the beach at

Tucker's Town are a spectacular feature developed from caves on the edge of the ocean and opened up by waves.

Page 89

MID OCEAN GOLF CLUB

Mid Ocean Club, which winds around Tucker's Town, is ranked among the top ten golf courses in the world by experts. Designed in 1924 by Charles Blair MacDonald and revised in 1953 by Robert Trent Jones, Mid Ocean's eighteen holes measure 6,519 yards and offer beautiful views over the ocean and romantic Tucker's Town.

Page 90

CRYSTAL CAVES

Bermuda's most beautiful caves are in the narrow strip of land between Harrington Sound and Castle Harbour. Leamington and Crystal Caves are outstanding, real underground wonderlands with stalagmites and stalactites, enhanced by crystal-clear pools of the subterranean fairyland.

Page 91

NIGHT LIFE IN BERMUDA – DANCING UNDER THE STARS

The balmy weather in Bermuda allows outside night life about the year around. There are also some very attractive night clubs, especially in the larger hotels, which offer a glittering variety of nightly entertainment, partly international, partly local. Bermuda is famed for its excellent native singers and musicians.

Page 92

PALM GROVE GARDEN (Devonshire)

The flower gardens of Bermuda are unique. The picture shows part of a private garden on South Road in Devonshire that is open to the public and noted for the variety of its arrangement.

RENTAL TRANSPORTATION

There are no rental cars in Bermuda, out of a desire to avoid too much traffic in the delightful narrow streets and roads of the islands. Taxis may be used for tourist transportation, and bicycles and Mobylettes (see picture) can be rented. The photograph shows a typical street scene, with the policeman directing traffic wearing Bermuda shorts, just as the tourists do.

(continued from page 72)

Hamilton City Hall. Officially opened in 1960, the fine City Hall is an imposing structure with its 91-foot tower, topped by a weather vane which is a replica of the Sea Venture. On the face of the tower is a colorful wind clock – the only one in Bermuda. This handsome center is not only an asset to the city, but indeed to the whole colony – providing a theater, lecture rooms, an art gallery (operated by the Bermuda Society of Arts) and Bermuda's new National Gallery. The Gallery opened in 1992 thanks to the dedicated work of many people and the gift of the Watlington art collection. The foyer and the administrative offices, especially the Mayor's Parlour, afford fine examples of local craftsmanship. The original Town Hall, an 18th-century building on Front Street East, now houses a court and Government offices.

Bermuda Cathedral. On the same street as the City Hall, atop a hill, the Bermuda Cathedral dominates the Hamilton skyline. Materials from as far away as Scotland, Normandy, Nova Scotia, and Indiana (U.S.A.) went into its construction, which bascially is of native stone. In all there are no less than ten churches of as many denominations in this little city, four of them on this Church Street.

Sessions House. Built in 1817 the Sessions House is on the highest hill in the city. The Supreme Court occupies the lower floor and the House of Assembly the upper floor. The Clock Tower was added in commemoration of Queen Victoria's Golden Jubilee and the clock struck for the first time at midnight, ushering out 1893 and welcoming 1894.

The Public Building. In this simple but dignified building, set in a park between Reid and Front Streets, are housed the Premier's Office, the Cabinet Office and the Senate Chamber. A number of portraits of Bermuda worthies grace the walls. It is here, too, that the opening and closing of Parliament takes place with colorful ceremony. Of much interest is the ancient cedar chair of Captain Josiah Forster, Governor in 1642. This historic piece is known as The Throne. The grounds around this building are well kept, the trees being of considerable age. Facing Front Street there is a small enclosure in which is the Cenotaph War Memorial, a replica of the one in Whitehall, London.

TOWARDS THE WEST

At the western end of Front Street is the Ferry Terminal, from which a little government ferry leaves on its westward journey to Ireland Island, where until 1951 the mighty Dockyard dominated life at the West End. Today the Royal Navy still retains a small base, but most of the splendid buildings are used for a superb shopping center, some interesting light factories and boatworks, and the Bermuda Maritime Museum. The Museum contains treasures found on Bermuda's reefs and has displays about the island's long maritime history and connection with the Royal Navy. A boat loft has a fully-rigged Bermuda fitted dinghy and a number of other wooden vessels preserved here as examples of the shipwright's work.

If you are getting about on a moped take it with you on the ferry and tour Somerset Island where the ferry makes a number of stops. There are many charming by-ways and a beautiful shoreline, and some fine examples of old Bermudian architecture.

Southwest of old Fort Scaur are the Cathedral Rocks, a natural formation which resembles gothic arches and pillars, all carved by the age-long pounding of the sea. In crossing from Somerset to the Main Island one crosses the world's smallest drawbridge, called Somerset Bridge, a rare sight when the oleanders are in bloom and a favorite subject for artists.

Returning to Hamilton by road, a visit to Gibb's Hill lighthouse is most rewarding as it affords the best view of the islands. Dramatic by day — romantic by moonlight — this slim, all white structure is said to have been only the second cast-iron lighthouse ever to have been built. Constructed between 1844-45 the light beamed for the first time on the 1st May, 1846.

SOUTH SHORE

From Southampton to Tucker's Town, along the South Shore Road there are numerous beaches, some of the most beautiful in the world, and breathtaking views, frequently through oleander hedges, of the surf breaking over the coral reef. Here, too, are located some of Bermuda's most luxurious hotels, clubs and cottage colonies.

PEMBROKE

On the northern side of Hamilton Harbour lies the largest and most populous parish, Pembroke. Beyond the city limits there are many beautiful roads leading through the fashionable residential areas of Pitt's Bay.

Fairylands and Point Shares. Further out is Spanish Point, so called because it is thought that it was here that the Spanish Captain Rameriz spent some three weeks repairing his ship which was stranded here in 1603.

St. John's Parish Church, first built in 1625, stands serene at the foot of Mount Langton, while the Rectory, the charming and every early 18th century house, Maria's Hill separates it from Government House. On the north shore, below Government House is the Black Watch well and the Ducking Stool. This latter was used as a form of correction in the early days for troublesome and over talkative wives.

TOWARDS THE EAST

As you travel east from Hamilton along the South Shore Road, visit the Botanical Gardens in Paget Parish. Here are Bermuda's infinite varieties of wonderful plants assembled in one spot. Next door is the small but up-to-date King Edward VII Memorial Hospital, which has affiliations with the foremost hospitals in Montreal. Further along is Verdmont in Smith's Parish. This elegant 18th-century Bermuda house has been completely restored and furnished with period furnishings by the Bermuda National Trust.

Inland, on Middle Road is Old Devonshire Church, dating back to 1716.

Again on the South Shore Road is Spanish Rock, already mentioned, and Spittal Pond, a bird sanctuary. From here it is easy to reach The

Devil's Hole—a deep natural fish pond where hungry groupers are an easy catch.

Further out is the Mid-Ocean Club whose golf course is said to be second only to St. Andrew's in Scotland. It is situated in Tucker's Town, Bermuda's most exclusive residential area, where in addition to Bermudians, wealthy Americans and Canadians have built splendid homes.

Circling northward around Harrington Sound one comes to a series of caves. Crystal Cave and Leamington Cave are the two open to visitors. Lighted by electricity, the crystal stalagmites and stalactites, formed by the dripping of water, for eons, assume weird and spectacular shapes. In the same area there is a cave called Prospero's, recalling Shakespeare's close association with several of the early Bermuda Adventurers: «The Tempest» was the happy outcome. The story goes that a carriage driver on pointing out this spot once said, «That cave is where Mr. Shakespeare went one time to shelter from a storm.»

The two most popular caves were discovered only some fifty years ago. One, when some children tried to recover a ball which had been lost by a small boy, they discovered instead one of Nature's true marvels. Careful electric lighting has made these caves veritable fairylands.

Completing the trip around Harrington Sound takes one past the Race Track and on to the Bermuda Government Aquarium situated on a narrow strip of land separating the Sound from Flatt's Inlet. Here is found the world's finest collection of tropical marine fish. Clean, cool and beautifully kept, the Aquarium provides a colorful display of specimens from Bermuda's offshore happy hunting grounds.

Adjoining the Aquarium is the Government Museum displaying much of interest in Natural History, handcrafts, old maps and recently has been added the fabulous and world famous Teddy Tucker Treasure. Next door there is a wonderful aviary of tropical birds which you are actually allowed to feed.

To arrive at picturesque Flatts Village across the colorful inlet you must cross a tiny bridge. Most probably the first spot to have been spanned by a bridge in Bermuda, this is the only outlet to the sea from Harrington Sound, and is a favorite fishing place. Flatts was once a thriving trading village, with sailing vessels tying up almost at the doors of the warehouse along the village street.

ST. GEORGE'S: COLONIAL TOWN

What you have so far seen and visited in the colony is present-day Bermuda with a sprinkling of 18th and 19th century homes and buildings.

As you approach the Town of St. George's, prepare yourself to step back in time to the 17th century. Founded in 1612, St. George's is the oldest continuous English settlement in the New World. It was the capital of Bermuda until 1815 when the government was transferred to Hamilton — at which time the town «went to sleep» so to speak and so retained undisturbed its peace and charm.

Today, with an ever expanding tourist industry, St. George's is coming to life once again. Always popular with visitors, there is now a conscious effort to make it one of Bermuda's principal attractions, although great care is being taken to retain the atmosphere of its colorful past. Restoration of old buildings is carried out with due regard to the original architecture.

Replicas of the stocks and pillory used in punishment in the 17th century have been placed on King's Square. Here, too, is the Town Hall, a comparatively modern building, built in 1808. Prior to this all official business was carried out in the State House, to be found to the east of the Square, and the oldest building still standing, having been built in 1620, the first to have been built entirely of stone. Originally it had a second storey where the powder was stored! When the government moved to Hamilton the State House became vested in the Corporation which has, since that date, rented it to Bermuda's oldest Freemason's Lodge, St. George 200, under the Scottish constitution (Charter 1797) for an annual rental of one peppercorn. The payment of this rent has become the occasion for a most colourful ceremony and one of the occasions when a Town Crier is used to lend atmosphere to the scene.

Even the street names of St. George's smoke the flavor of English Colonial days... One Gun Alley, Old Maid's Lane, Shinbone Alley, Blockade Alley, King's Square, Printer's Alley. Some of the streets and lanes are so narrow that even Bermuda's midget cars have difficulty entering them and it is best to explore the town on foot.

Around the corner from King's Square is Duke of York Street – St. George's shopping center. York Street is particularly famous for St. Peter's Church, which is the oldest Anglican Church in the Western Hemisphere. The first wooden church built by Governor Moore in 1612 was blown down, but a more substantial building was erected in 1619 by Governor Butler. It was on this site that the present church was rebuilt in 1713 and enlarged in 1814. Its present restoration has been carefully and lovingly carried out during the past few years. The cedar altar was in use in 1624; the communion silver was donated by King

William III in 1697. An even older piece of silver is a small chalice sent out by the Bermuda Company in 1625 and bearing the Company Seal, probably purchased with a legacy from Sir Thomas Smith, the Treasurer.

Across the street is a sleepy little house now known as the Globe Confederate Museum. During the American Civil War it was the home of the Political Agent of the Confederacy and therefore the very hub of the high adventure of the days of blockade-running out of Bermuda. Even then the house was old and had known a stormy history. Built by Governor Samuel Day in the garden of the too dilapidated old Government House between 1698–1700, this pompous gentleman claimed it to be his own. Before this dispute was settled, Day had been replaced, imprisoned in the King's Castle and had died. Finally, it was awarded to his heir-at-law who had the audacity to offer it for sale to the government to serve as the much needed Government House.

Behind St. Peter's facing Broad Alley is the «Old Rectory», now the Public Library. This little gem of early Bermuda architecture was the very early 18th century home of one George Dew, a reformed and pardoned pirate of Rhode Island. Dew later became a respected citizen of St. George's: a church warden, assemblyman, and judge of the court of Vice-Admiralty. Mid-century it became the «rectory» when Bermuda's most colorful parson, the Rev. Alexander Richardson, known as the «little bishop», married the widowed lady whose home it was.

While visiting St. George's, do not miss the replica of the Deliverance on Ordnance Island, one of two ships built by the Sea Venture survivors. Other points of interest include 18th-century Tucker House on Water Street with its fine collection of antique furniture; the Carriage House on the same street, fronting the charming Somers Wharf shopping area; the St. George's Historical Society Museum on Duke of Kent Street; and the

Featherbed Alley printing press in the Museum's cellar.

Near a corner of the Somers Garden on Duke of York St. was buried the heart of Bermuda's founder – Sir George Somers. A little park and a simple stone column perpetuate his memory.

HISTORIC FORTS

St. George's is ringed by forts – some of them erected during early colonial days when Spanish adventurers travelled the seas. The first is Gates' Fort built in 1612. Here above the fort flies the old flag of England, showing only the crosses of St. George and St. Andrew. The cross of St. Patrick was not added until the year 1801. Next is Fort St. Catherine whose foundations were constructed in 1613. The huge pile of masonry seen today is the result of the great fortification works carried out at the end of 18th century and again between the 1860s and 1880, when Bermuda indeed became the «Gibraltar of the West». This fort offers a beautiful view of the sea and Sea Venture Flat where Sir George Somers was shipwrecked.

Beyond the fort lies Tobacco Bay. It was from this bay that the gunpowder was loaded into small boats and taken to the American ships waiting off shore on the night of the infamous (or famous, depending on your loyalties) raid on the magazine to aid the armies of Washington in 1775. Up the hill is the Gunpowder Cavern, a beautifully restored powder magazine of much later date – built somewhere in the vicinity of the earlier site of the theft.

The pleasant task of encircling Bermuda is completed by taking a trip to St. David's Island and visiting St. David's Lighthouse at the colony's extreme eastern tip. Off this St. David's Head is the finishing line for the Newport to Bermuda Ocean Yacht Race. From here the view is superb and the feeling of being in the middle of the Atlantic Ocean becomes very real. From here, too, can be seen the ruins of Bermuda's oldest and most important forts, as well as the vast air defense base built by the U.S. during World War II.

St. David's Islanders formerly were among the most picturesque of all Bermudians. This no doubt was due to their isolation – the Severn Bridge, joining St. David's to St. George's, was not opened until 1934. The colored inhabitants are reputed to be the descendants of Indians, Negroes and Irish ancestors. The end of an era was forced on the islanders with the building of Kindley Air Force Base, known then as Fort Bell. Today the Civil Airport is at the western end of the base.

The Square of St. George's, Bermuda, 1823.

THE PEOPLE OF BERMUDA

Although Bermuda entertains thousands of visitors, Bermudians are not a race of innkeepers and waiters. Tremendously hospitable though they may be – and the native institution of the «Guest House» proves that throughout the islands – the contemporary Bermudian is more likely to be «in trade» although he may count among his ancestors hardy colonial seafarers and adventurous settlers. All the «best people» make up, in effect, a merchant aristocracy.

For the most part the descendants of the old Bermuda families are conservative, proud of being a part of the British Commonwealth and devoted to preserving the beauty, the status quo and the economy of their native isle. In Bermuda there are no direct income taxes and only a small public debt, and most years the budget is carefully balanced.

Bermuda is a British colony but has always enjoyed a high degree of self-government. With the change in the constitution in 1968 self-government moved to a different stage. Bermuda took responsibility for all aspects of government except foreign affairs, and internal and external security. These were reserved to Britain and are normally administered by His Excellency the Governor, who is appointed by London, and his local council. The legislature consists of the lower House of Assembly, whose members are elected, and the upper House, the Senate. The members of the Senate are appointed by the leaders of the two leading political parties and the Governor in such a way that if all opposition and Governor-appointed independent Senators vote against a measure they can defeat it by one vote. Voters must be over the age of 18.

Conservatism and a love of tradition go hand in hand – particularly in Bermuda. The House of Assembly, first convened in 1620, is presided over by a bewigged Speaker. Wigs are the rule in the Bermuda Supreme Court where at the beginning of each session the ancient Silver Oar, emblem of the Court of Vice-Admiralty, is carried into the Court and placed on the bench in front of the Chief Justice. This oar, of which there are only six in the world, is older than the one used in Probate, Divorce and Admiralty division of the High Court of Justice in England by more than a century, having been made probably prior to 1700. It has been in Bermuda since about that date.

Bermudians celebrate some unusual holidays – Bermuda Day (formerly Empire Day), the Queen's birthday, and Cup Match/Somers Day, a two-day holiday when cricket teams representing the ends of the island vie with each other for an historic silver cup.

There were no aboriginal inhabitants. Bermudians of today descend from three main sources which are increasingly blending. The original English settlers came first in 1612, to be followed in 1616 by the first Negro and the first Amerindian. Although some Negroes came directly from Africa, others were brought from the West Indies and even England. The Indians came from both North America and the Caribbean. Another European group brought to Bermuda were Portuguese, who came as gardeners mainly from the Azores. Generally speaking all groups get on well together and have taken the island's gradual change in economic emphasis from tourism to off-shore companies in their stride.

To a small extent the folklore of Africa has penetrated to Bermuda with the dancing of the «Gombeys». These colorfully costumed groups parade the streets to the beat of drums on Boxing Day and Easter Monday. Over the last 50 or 60 years many negroes have migrated to Bermuda from the West Indies, bringing with them the calypso rhythm and more recently the music of the steel drum.

BERMUDA HOMES

The island's unique homes have been the delight of architects and visitors. White-roofed and washed pastel hues of pink and blue, Bermuda's houses delight the tourist eye with their tropical appearance, particularly when they have enclosed gardens aflame with bougainvillea, red hibiscus, royal poinciana or Easter lilies.

Buildings made of native limestone replaced the earlier half-timbered houses, which in turn supplanted the first huts with cedar walls and palmetto roofs. Nowadays concrete or «breeze» blocks generally made on the island are used; these, when covered with stucco, look the same as limestone houses.

The use of stone meant that the material for a home was often hewn from the property, the resulting excavation being used for a quarry garden or for a cistern or tank beneath the building. Bermuda has no rivers or springs so tanks are important as most houses provide their own water supply. The water is caught on the roof, nearly always made of limestone, with stone gutters to lead the rain to down-pipes for the tank. The system works well, so development of a piped water supply has been slow. It is based on water drawn from marshes and on freshwater found permeating the rock of the island just above sea level.

Before refrigeration, every house had its «buttery». This strange pyramidal-shaped structure was used for the storage of food in hot weather and was always detached from the house. Today, these are used as studios, beach houses and even, when joined to the main house, as bathrooms.

Bermuda homes have been described as being basically English cottages adapted to the specific and unique conditions existing in Bermuda. Handsome examples of gracious 18th century Bermuda homes—such as Verdmont and the Tucker House—are open to the public.

APPEARANCE AND ORIGIN

Mention of Bermuda to those who know the islands evokes the image of curving pink-sand beaches backed by shell-gray rocks, gently rolling hills, and dunes—all surrounded by a turquoise sea. The coloring is that of El Greco. Bermuda is a tiny citadel of beauty alone in the vast Atlantic. The nearest land is Cape Hatteras, 568 miles due west, in North Carolina. Bermuda is 2,950 miles from Liverpool, England. Because the first mariners were so surprised to find this lonely speck of land in the ocean, without any apparent reason for its being, Bermuda emerges into history clouded with myth.

There are seven chief islands and about 131 smaller ones large enough to have been named. The group is attenuated, it arcs into a fish-hook, and the seven principal islands are linked by bridges. They are, from east to west, St. George's, St. David's, the Main Island, Somerset, Watford, Boaz, and Ireland. The total area is 20.59 square miles. The chain of islands is fifteen miles long and two and a half miles wide at its greatest width.

One of the fascinating things about Bermuda is that it is unique in appearance, flavor, and geography. If you had ever been there and were transported back by magic or a dream, you would immediately recognize that you were on Bermuda and nowhere else, even though you might have no landmarks or man-made structures to guide you in recognition. Palm trees flourish in the frost-free air, but this is not one of the tropical clusters of islands in the West Indies. Underlying the land is an old, extinct volcano, but there are no volcanic peaks rising into rain forests in the clouds. It is a rolling land, fertile in the valleys and on the lower slopes. The word that applies to the landscape of Bermuda is «gentle.»

This is not true of the skyscape, which derives from the land. The clouds that float above the little specks of land are formed by them, and these towering cumulus shapes and feathery cirrus that ride the winds above them can only be called «noble». There are no sunsets more beautiful than those of Bermuda.

The sea may be as blue in some other favored spots, but nowhere is it bluer than in Bermuda. The seascapes give Bermuda its strength. All that marvelous blue Atlantic, unbroken all the way to the Canary Islands, comes surging in against the reefs and boulders that guard the pink-sand beaches — and the sea does not wear the islands down, it builds them up, on the whole.

Another thing that fascinates one about these islands is that, though they are so small, they give the effect of diversity. They have individual personalities. They can be explored with never-failing delight. This is because of the curving hills, the looping, intertwining shoreline, and the caves.

In its geological origin, Bermuda is not unique. The islands and the banks that lie round them are volcanic in origin and have other counterparts in the Atlantic and the Pacific. They are the peak of a volcanic ridge that began to rise from the floor of the ocean a hundred million years ago. In this they resemble the Lesser Antilles, Iceland, and the Azores. However, they have a limestone cap, and in this respect they are similar to the Bahamas.

When the cone of the volcano that was to become Bermuda reached above the ocean, it began to be eroded by waves and rain. Around the cone, just beneath the surface, a platform of eroded volcanic sand was formed. On the platform grew coral caps, and in the sand and along the beaches there were many molluscs. Shells became limestone sand, and the stone rose above the volcanic sands. In time, a thick cap of limestone and limey sandstone covered the old volcanic cone. The volcanic rock that is the base of the islands lies far beneath the sea's surface. Today Bermuda is on the northern margin of the Atlantic area in which coral grows, but in many eras in the past, when the seas were warmer, the coral colonies that extract lime from the sea and build the hard coral rock proliferated.

Much of Bermuda's surface rock is what is called aeolian limestone. This is formed when the wind piles limey sand into dunes and the rain cements the sand and lime into rock. What resulted in Bermuda is unusual. The sand piled into dunes by the wind and called calciferous sand is made from the particles of shell and old coral rock. This material tends to dissolve in the heavy rains. During the ice ages the water seeping into the sand carried sufficient calcium to cement the dunes into a rock that is named **aeolianite.** This is the stone that is so widely used as a building material.

Again and again during the ages, when the glaciers melted and re-formed and the ocean rose and fell, this limestone-forming process went on. When the islands were above the sea, the rocks would weather, plants would grow, and soil would form. Geologists find in Bermuda a beautiful record of what went on in shore formations in the Ice Ages.

In Bermuda, bays and sounds curve in and around and between the islands and the rocks. Long lines of hills curve around ponds and marshes. There are no rivers or streams, nor is there any evidence that there ever have been. The lowlands are the result of the development of sinkholes between ridges. This kind of topography is called Karst, for the Karst region of Yugoslavia consists of limestone in which basins and caves have been scoured out. Because of the heavy rainfall, the summits of the hills have had the soil washed away, and they are usually rather bare of vegetation.

The surface stone is so porous that water flows through it under the island from the sea while rain water seeps down through the rock and floats on the salt. The fresh water layer is thickest in the middle of the island and is called the lens. The existence of this supply of water, available through vertical wells, was only discovered after the Second World War – in part thanks to a man with a dowsing rod, Henry Gross, who was brought to the island by the author, Kenneth Roberts. Before that an ingenious system of providing the Hamilton area with water was developed by the entrepreneur, Sir Henry Watlington, who drew fresh water from the top of Devonshire Marsh through horizontal wells. Water obtained by this system and then treated still serves the Hamilton area and several parishes.

The limestone of Bermuda is a rigid sponge. Where plants grow and die, humus is formed. When rain falls on this humus as it decays, humic acid is formed. When the acid percolates into limestone rocks, it dissolves some of the lime. This is the way in which the topographical features of Bermuda were formed. In most limey regions of the world where the process has gone on, streams, rivers and lakes have been brought into being. But in Bermuda, because the islands are so very narrow and porous, there is no fresh water on the surface, but valleys, sinkholes, and caves have been shaped by the percolation of the rain. The eroded valleys and the bottoms of the sinkholes have rapidly become filled with alluvial soil, sand, and humus, and this soil is fertile.

One of the most memorable aspects of Bermuda is its pink sand. It does not take a specialist to determine that much of this sand is shelly in origin. Sift it through your fingers on the beach and you will see the shell particles. Because of the prevailing winds and waves, the South Shore is the sandiest. Coral reefs contribute their share of sand to the land also, and much of the beauty to the waters around Bermuda. Coral grows in the shallow waters off land masses in the tropical and sub-tropical world, and nowhere farther north than Florida around the continental United States today. But living coral grows around Bermuda. The reefs protect the land, shelter the fish, and delight undersea explorers. The warm Gulf Stream that crosses the Atlantic nearby is responsible for this blessing. Along the South Shore of Bermuda are coral atolls known as «pot boilers». The living coral rises around the rim of the atoll in a circle, and the sunken hollow in the center has been worn by circulating water into the underlying limestone.

In terms of geological eras, the North Shore of Bermuda is youthful, the South Shore mature. The youthful coast is steep, rocky, not worn away by sea and wind. The mature coast has been planed smooth by time and tide and has sandy shores deposited by the ocean in past millennia.

CAVES, COVES AND COAST

Bermuda's limestone is honeycombed with caves, underground amphitheaters with floors almost one hundred feet beneath the surface of the land. In the shapes sculptured by nature and in the coloring of the formations and deposits within the caves, they are a delight to the eye and the imagination. Transparently clear salt water pools have been formed in the caves by seepage and underground passages to the sea. Some are open to the public and have electric lights showing the way into the caverns. Many more are on land not open to the public and are hidden by vegetation.

The geological account of the formation of these caves is more fascinating than any myth, for measurements indicate that some have been far more than half a million years in the making; the sea has risen and fallen several times during their creation. They have been carved from the rock by that percolating, slightly acid water that dissolves the limestone, as most caves have been created in other regions of the world. The water has eaten away one part of the stone and not another, because some of the stone is harder, denser, and more tightly cemented than are other adjacent strata of rock. It is also evident in some parts of the island that hollow sand pockets exist under the cap of limestone. The softer rock and the sand have been washed out, in a process that went on more rapidly during the Ice Ages than it does now. During those times much more of the ocean's waters were locked in the ice caps that spread out from both poles. The seas of the world fell far below the level at which they now stand, not once but several times.

More rain fell in that cold time. Bermuda was more elevated above the sea, so the washing out of soft stone and sandy pockets under the stone cap went on more rapidly then than it does now.

After the caves were formed, they were adorned with stalactites and stalagmites. The water would drip down into a cavern ever so slowly; as a drop fell from the roof, it left behind a little of the lime dissolved in it. When it landed on the floor of the cave, it deposited a little lime before evaporating or flowing away to the sea. In that way stalactites and stalagmites were formed, as ages wheeled past. A stalactite hangs down from the ceiling of the caves, like a flow of water suddenly turned to stone in mid-air. A stalagmite grows up from the floor of the caves as the lime crystallizes out of the fallen water.

Not only are the shapes of the dripping stone exotic, the coloring is also most beautiful and the surfaces often sensuously smooth to the touch. Some stones are pale white, others are red or tinged with green from iron or copper dissolved in the waters that formed them.

Some of the caves have been rich in finds of fossil birds. A study of the fossil bones shows that the birds had been unable to fly when they were alive.

Among the dramatic big caves that are open to the public are the Crystal Caves in Hamilton Parish, near the Causeway. The underground scenery is well lighted with electric lights, and steps have been cut in the rocks. The stalactites drip from the roof into Crystal Lake, a clear pool of salt water that rises and falls with the tide and is about thirty feet deep at the height of the incoming sea. A pontoon bridge allows the explorer to enjoy the whole stone forest of stalactites and stalagmites.

Nearby are a number of other caverns — Leamington Cave, Cahow Cave, Castle Grotto, Blue Hole, and Fern Cave. Another is Cathedral

Cave, with a mighty stalagmite that looks like an organ pipe. Leamington Cave is near Harrington Sound and just off Sound Road. With its arched dome more than sixty feet underground, it is truly out of this world. This double-chambered cave is also well lighted. In Castle Grotto Cave the visitor can enjoy the glittering roof above the fish-filled waters of its pool, Blue Hole.

Fascinating evidence of the ages that it took to create the great caves is found in the record of a stalagmite from Walsingham Cave. This huge stone column, eleven feet high, was cut in 1819 and sent to a museum in Edinburgh, Scotland. A measurement made years later of the tiny new stalagmites forming on the stump of the big one indicated that, at the rate they were growing, it took 600,000 years of dripping to create the stalagmite taken from Bermuda to Scotland.

When a cave becomes geologically old, it may collapse, and what is left has its own special fascination. The roof falls in, leaving arches of rock, strange columns, and limpid pools of great beauty, known prosaically as sinks. The death of a cave formed the dramatic natural arch of rock near the Mid-Ocean Club at Tucker's Town beside the beach. The islands are graced with all sorts of fantastic natural rock sculpture that originated in the collapse of caves, and the land near the shores is dotted with clear sinks filled with salt water that enters through underground passages or through seepage. Cathedral Rocks is a noble ruin of a natural temple formed during the process of cave-making and cave-dying, with the added help of wave erosion.

One of them, Devil's Hole, has been one of Bermuda's most distinctive attractions for more than a century. It is a land-locked, crystal-clear, salt-water pool filled with fish — a natural aquarium. There is apparently no connection between the waters of Devil's Hole, which are about thirty feet deep, and nearby Harrington Sound, and presumably the sea fills this marine pool through an undersea channel from the South Shore of the island.

Here, more than a thousand strange and beautiful fish serenely glide through the clear waters, thronging to the surface when they are fed. Angel Fish, grouper, rockfish, and many other colorful reef fish make their home here. Visitors are allowed to fish for them — with a baited line but without a hook. Devil's Hole earned its name because of the strange growling noise that the water makes at very low tide when, probably, it passes underground between the sink and the sea. The word has, quite naturally, become «Go to Devil's Hole and see the Angel Fish.» Like other sinks, it was once a large cave, as stalactites and stalagmites attest, and in its present form was created when the roof caved in.

The reefs and patches of coral near the coasts are another source of great pleasure, especially in these days of SCUBA diving and undersea tourism. The coral canyons are home to a multitude of fish and other sea creatures, and purple sea fans wave. To float above the canyons on the surface of the water and watch this world through a face mask is to be relaxed. To dive is to explore a beauty the land cannot offer. For those who don't want to get wet, there are glass-bottomed boats to take them to the sea gardens near the coast.

THE CLIMATE

The climate is the chief asset of Bermuda, making it a haven for refugees from winter. It is so breeze-washed that sunlovers enjoy it in the summer, too. Warmed by the nearby Gulf Stream, the islands have not had a frost since official weather records have been kept. Sunstroke is also unknown here.

The surrounding ocean warms the specks of land in the winter and cools them in the summer. The climate is subtropical, though Bermuda is opposite Cape Hatteras in North Carolina. South Florida can get colder than Bermuda has ever been. There is not a great range of temperature throughout the year. The lowest temperature ever officially recorded in Bermuda was 41 degrees. The average temperature in August, the hottest month, is 80 degrees, and in February, the coolest, 62 degrees. The bitter winter cold fronts that move from Canada and New England over the ocean toward Bermuda are warmed by the Gulf Stream before they reach the islands, where they bring rain but never snow.

The weather of Bermuda does change, and in a delightful fashion. After several clear blue days, cumulus clouds tower high, sweep across the land, and shed showers, and then the sun comes out again and a fresh, air-conditioning breeze springs up. There is nothing dull or listless about the weather. Connoisseurs of skyscapes are among Bermuda's most devoted lovers. The frequent changes in winds and the brief, heavy rain showers are brought about by the great pattern of winds that prevails in the Atlantic.

A dominant weather feature of the Atlantic is the «Azores-Bermuda high.» This «high» is an air mass composed of winds circulating clockwise around a high-pressure center. The high-pressure system normally lies over the ocean between Bermuda and the Azores, and its movement gives Bermuda its refreshing changes in weather. Movement of the high-pressure system north and south determines Bermuda's winds and showers, and the high is so situated that Bermuda frequently lies in what is called a zone of convergence. In this zone the trade winds blowing from the east that dominate the ocean south of Bermuda meet the winds coming from the west that have crossed the continent of North America.

The pattern of weather in the summer depends on the movement of the high-pressure system lying over the ocean to the east. When the high moves toward the Azores, the easterly trade winds curve round it and bring to Bermuda clear and sunny days and bright blue skies. Then, usually, the high migrates again, and the winds shift toward the south, bringing high clouds and rain showers. It is the convergence of winds from the high-pressure system with those of a low-pressure system moving toward Bermuda from the west that produces the frequent showers. The prevailing winds of the islands are from the south, southwest, and west. The occasional storms with high winds that pass over Bermuda come in the fall. Bermuda has a yearly average of 7.1 hours of sunshine a day. Though the air is moist, the average humidity is less than that of Britain. There is no dry season in the islands, and the brief, heavy rains refresh the land throughout the year. There is no rainy season, either, no periods when one is shut in all day. The welcome rain keeps the islands emerald green, and Bermudians catch some of it to store in stone reservoirs or tanks for their water supply. The entire absence of fog over the islands is one of the most welcome aspects of the climate. There are no heat waves. The sea temperature is warmer than the land in the winter, cooler in the summer. The outdoor life is pleasant all the year round.

Because of the benign weather, visitors have been going to Bermuda to recuperate from illnesses, including nervous prostration, since before the time there was a United States. The cold of the northeastern United States and Canada, which brought on pneumonia, could be avoided here, and English colonists in North America quickly learned this. It did not take the English long, either, to realize that the climate of Bermuda is kinder than that of the Riviera and other Mediterranean lands. The islands are also a refuge for those suffering from hay fever.

Relaxing is the word for a land where warm rains nurture roses and violets in midwinter.

VEGETATION OF BERMUDA

The first settlers of Bermuda found a dense covering of vegetation, with the famous cedar trees dominating the landscape. The subtropical forests and swamps were lush. Wind, water, and birds carried the seeds of the first plants to the specks of land soon after they rose above the sea.

The fragrant Bermuda cedar, a species of juniper, is an evergreen tree. It grows both on rock and on fertile soils. Because the wood is superior for boatbuilding and for furniture-making, it was highly valued and heavily timbered. However, since 1945 most of the Bermuda cedars have been killed by a scale pest, in spite of strenuous attempts to eradicate the disease. New cedars are growing, and there is hope for a revival.

Seeds of the palmetto tree were also brought in by natural agencies in the distant past, and the first colonists found these tall and striking emigrants from the southern part of the United States raising their distinctive crowns on the islands. The colonists not only ate the delectable heart of the palmetto and used its leaves to thatch their shelters, they also used the palmetto sap to make a potent fermented alcoholic drink called «bibby». Not nearly so many palmettos are found on Bermuda today as once flourished there, but they can be seen on the North Shore in Palmetto Park, around Paget Marsh, and in Devonshire on the South Shore.

The bay grape, also called the sea grape, is one of the most handsome of Bermuda's native trees. Its seeds are viable in salt water, and they grow on the dunes of many tropical and subtropical lands. It has large, shiny, almost round leaves and a handsome, many-branching trunk with a thin bark that varies from red to brown. The «grapes» that hang from these trees in the fall are not particularly tasty, but a good jelly can be made from them.

Another native tree, the mangrove, is strange to northerners but familiar to anyone who has lived in tropical or subtropical climes around the world. The mangrove seed floats in on the tide, drops its heavier end down, and roots on tidal flats. It requires some salt in the water in which it grows. The glossy-leafed trees put out many, many roots into the air and then down into the water and the soil. These roots catch sand and silt and bind them down, so the trees have a great reputation as land builders in warm climates. The waters that flow about their roots are nurseries for all sorts of infant sea creatures. Mangrove blooms make an excellent honey.

The purple morning-glory vines grow luxuriantly over the wastelands of the islands and can strangle trees. One of the most attractive of the native Bermuda plants is the Bermudiana, a small thing with lovely blue flowers bearing a yellow eye. It resembles the iris and blooms profusely on rocky hillsides and near sandy shores in early summer. There is also a maidenhair fern that has become abundant on walls and cliffs. Magnificent giant ferns with stalks five feet long are found in some marshes. The Spanish bayonet is another native plant, easy to identify. It has many long, stiff, heavy leaves, bearing sharp points, and most dramatic and delicate white blooms that contrast sharply with the stiff plant.

Over the centuries since men first settled on the islands, the vegetation of Bermuda has, of course, changed. The heavy mantle of cedar has gone, but much that is beautiful has been added. This is because the climate has been hospitable to both temperate and tropical plants. Oleanders, originally from the Mediterranean but introduced from South Carolina, casuarina trees from Australia, roses from China — all are at home there now. Bananas, coconut palms, royal poincianas, royal palms, passion flowers, Easter lilies, orange trees, peach trees all thrive. Bamboo graces the landscape frequently. Pungent lantana grows wild. Some cactus is native to the island, other decorative varieties have been introduced and grow well. One of the most beautiful members of the cactus family is the night-blooming cereus, which bears a magnificent and fragrant flower that never lasts beyond the dawn. Mimosas and acacias have made themselves at home, growing well even when neglected. Poinsettias bloom outdoors at Christmas time (if the plants have been pruned at the proper time). Hibiscus shrubs

Cedar Avenue, Hamilton, 1885

add the bright notes of their red, pink, and yellow flowers to the landscape and are prized as hedges. Many species of ficus trees thrive, and the rubber tree is one of them.

The most distinctive thing about the vegetation of Bermuda, to visitors from colder climates, is that there is no fall, no winter, no time of bare, gray branches. The leaves of the trees and shrubs and vines are pushed off after new leaves have grown. It is an evergreen world. Both to the botanist interested in introducing plants from other parts

131

of the world and to the gardener with a green thumb, Bermuda is a delectable part of the world, for a great variety of vegetation will do well there, given the proper care.

The Famous
Bermuda Flower Gardens

Because Bermuda has proved to be as hospitable to trees and flowers of the world as it is to people, the gardens are a joy. Here the beloved blooms of England, the roses and delphiniums, thrive alongside orchids and begonias. Because Bermudians and their visitors live outdoors the year round, gardens are greatly cherished as outdoor living rooms.

For decades one of the most beautiful sights on the islands has been the vast expanse of Easter lilies that are grown for export. First it was the bulbs that were raised for the market, back in the nineteenth century. Later, but before the days of air freight, blooms were shipped. Today, in the jet age, not only lilies but many other flowers are flown to market in the northeastern United States. The open fields of flowers that bloom when frost still threatens on the North American continent are breathtaking.

The great variety of native and imported decorative trees and plants can be seen in the Public Garden at St. George's and at the Agricultural Station at Paget. The traditional English love for gardening has also resulted in enriching the landscape. Sea captains brought back roses from the Orient, begonias from Mexico, orchids from Central America, Mexico, the West Indies, and Asia. If the right species of orchid is selected for a Bermuda garden, it demands less attention than many other plants. Calendula thrive here. Date palms grow well. Honeysuckle perfumes the air. Nasturtiums and passion flowers are among the favorites.

All gardeners, it has been said, plant the gardens of their memories. That is why so many of the blooming borders and beds that grace Bermuda gardens evoke England and New England. But there is a hunger, too, among those who love a world in bloom, to experiment with new and exotic color and fragrance. One of the favorite imported trees that have become domesticated on the islands is the royal poinciana, also known as flamboyant. It is a handsome shade tree in summer, with its high umbrella-shaped crown and lacy little green leaves. In May it bursts into bloom and is like a fountain of flame.

Backyard fruit gardens are also found throughout the islands. Bananas, grapefruit, oranges, avocadoes, peaches, and loquats are grown for home consumption.

GOLFING IN BERMUDA

With due apologies to Scotland, many widely-traveled golfers feel that Bermuda is the most perfect place to pursue their sport. Here the fairways are forever green, and the only complaint about them is that the views along the courses can be distracting. There are eight golf courses on the islands. Only two are private clubs which require an introduction by a member or by a hotel.

The Port Royal Golf Course, which is Bermuda's largest course, is by the sea in Southampton. It is one of two government-owned courses, the other being the Ocean View Golf Course overlooking the North Shore in Devonshire. Port Royal, laid out by golf architect Robert Trent Jones, rivals the Mid Ocean Golf Course, considered by experts to be one of the top ten in the world. The Mid Ocean was designed in 1924 by Charles Blair MacDonald, and revised by Robert Trent Jones in 1953. It winds beside the Atlantic for 6,547 yards compared with Port Royal's 6,565 yards.

The first course on Bermuda was that of Riddell's Bay Golf and Country Club, designed in 1922 by Devereux Emmett. It is so near the ocean that youngsters make money by diving for golf balls. Belmont Golf Club is the second oldest on the islands. The fairways of the eighteen holes beside the Great Sound are fringed with oleanders and casuarinas.

The third largest course on Bermuda is that of the Castle Harbour Golf Club. Its eighteen holes, amidst spectacular scenery, were designed on rolling hills by Charles Banks and redesigned by Robert Trent Jones. The Princess Golf and Beach Club has an eighteen-hole executive course on high ground that is well watered and in perfect shape throughout the year. It was designed by golf architect Alfred H. Tull. Near St. George's is the eighteen-hole, well-manicured St. George's Golf Club Course, also laid out by Robert Trent Jones, and the newest in Bermuda.

FISHING

Bermuda is a favorite base for sports fishermen, for it offers great angling along the shore, above the coral reefs, and in the deep, blue waters around the islands. A fleet of fine charter boats is based here, at Somerset, Southampton, Pembroke, Paget, Smith's Parish, and St. George's. They are well equipped, with outriggers, fighting chairs, and experienced crews. The fishing season lasts from May through November, and during that time some of the best light-tackle fishing anywhere in the world can be found in the surrounding waters.

The Annual Bermuda Game Fishing Tournament starts on January 1 and ends on December 31. The tournament is run under the rules of the Bermuda Game Fishing Association. No entry fee and no fishing licenses are required. There are seven categories of tackle, ranging from 2-pound test to 30-pound test. Bermuda also gives a Certificate of Release for game fish that are let go. The contest is limited to fish taken by amateur fishermen with rod and reel. All fish must be officially entered, and the captain of any charter boat can explain how this is done.

In the deep waters offshore the fisherman who is looking for a fight with the larger game fish can be pretty sure to find one. The real heavy-weight here is the Allison tuna, also known as the yellowfin tuna. Tunas are taken offshore either by trolling or by chumming, and nothing in the sea can stage such a battle on light tackle.

Wahoo, the speed demons that are among the top ten game fish of the world, run in mid-May. Some are boated throughout the summer. Then, in September and October, the major run is on, and it is hard not to catch a wahoo at that time. They are hooked near St. George's off the eastern end of the islands, and on Challenger Bank and Argus Bank.

Quite a few record-breaking blackfin tuna, which are great fighters, have been caught off Bermuda. In the water over the banks, world-record amberjack have also been caught. Horse-eye bonito and oceanic bonito put up a good fight. Dolphin (the fish, not the smiling mammal) make an especially thrilling catch because they are so beautiful. «Parting day dies like the dolphin» is an accurate description, for they turn sunset colors before expiring. False albacore is another lively catch found in the deeper waters.

Around the twenty square miles of land in Bermuda lie two hundred square miles of coral reef. The reefs are home to a wide variety of fish. Some put up a great fight, some make great eating. They are a perennial source of pleasure to the light-tackle fishermen in outboard-powered small boats. Some of the deep-water fish also cruise about the reefs, such as false albacore, amberjack, and horse-eye bonito. Yellowtails and gray snappers are found in abundance. Down on the bottom, living in caves, are groupers, which make a splendid chowder.

Along the shore in shallow water swims one of the world's greatest small-game fish, the bonefish. Fishing for bonefish along the beaches in clear, hip-deep water is the favorite sport of many experienced fishermen. All the beauty of that world is suddenly enlivened by a strike by one of the finest fighters of them all. A number of world-record bonefish have been taken around Bermuda. Another great fish that is often caught from the beach by surf fishermen is the pompano, which frequents the waters along the South Shore. Pompano are not only a gourmet's delight, they put up a brisk fight on light tackle. The gray or mangrove snapper is found lurking along the shore and among the roots of the mangrove trees. The angler who catches one of these fish can consider himself really expert, for they are most wily and suspicious.

TREASURE DIVING

Tales to delight a dreaming boy are told of treasure diving round Bermuda. Between pirates and storms, ships bearing fortunes undoubtedly were sunk in these waters. What the treasure hunter looks for when he explores undersea with SCUBA outfit or by helmet diving are ballast rocks and straight lines. The ballast rocks are piles of river-washed stone, obviously out of place in the sea and often all that is visible of an old sunken ship. The straight lines may mean cannon or keels, for the sea is not given to forming straight lines naturally. Today experienced divers scan the water around Bermuda with metal-detecting devices and by eye from helium balloons and small aircraft flying low and slow.

Teddy Tucker, born in Paget, Bermuda, in 1925, is living proof that treasure can be found. In his youth he became a proficient diver and in World War II the Royal Navy found good use for his proficiency. He went into commercial diving in 1949, and in 1955 he came up with a magnificent gold and emerald cross from the Spanish ship **San Pedro,** lost on Bermuda's north reefs in the fall of 1594. Since then the sea has given up more than a million dollars' worth of treasure to him from wrecks of the past four centuries. Treasure divers today comb the archives of Europe for clues as to what sank where and when. The nice thing about undersea treasure hunting off Bermuda is that the day is not lost when you find nothing — the scenery is so beautiful.

The 350th Anniversary
of Bermuda's Parliament

In 1970 Bermuda pridefully celebrated the 350th anniversary of the Bermuda Parliament, the first Parliament in the western world, and the oldest in the present world next to those of Britain and Iceland. The islanders have taken to hear the dictum «Mankind has two alternatives: Free and orderly discussion in Parliament with majority rule or fighting in the streets.»

The first self-government in Bermuda was carried on by a House of Assembly, which first met in 1620 after the burgesses had sworn an oath that they would transact their business with impartiality and «due secrecy.» This first Parliament passed fifteen bills, made plans to build bridges, protect wild life, inspect tobacco, and hold assizes twice a year to punish criminals. The governor, appointed by the Adventurers of the Virginia Company who had founded the colony, presided, and the company approved all the initial laws. This first Parliament met on August 1, 1620, in St. Peter's Church in St. George's. In the same year the building of a Sessions House, now the oldest structure on the islands, began. Rough-cut limestone blocks two feet thick were used for the walls, and they were cemented together with a mortar made of lime and turtle oil.

When the capital of Bermuda was moved to Hamilton from St. George's in 1815, the House of Assembly first met in the Customs House Warehouse. This was built in 1794, and its most recent role has been as a fire station. A new Sessions House was completed on a crest overlooking the harbor in 1826. It is still part of the larger Sessions House in which Parliament meets today. Two old pieces of statuary that once graced Westminster Palace walls and a heraldic lion from Britain stand at the entrance to the Sessions House. The Assembly meets on the second floor and the Supreme Court on the first floor. The Speaker's gavel used today was made from Bermuda cedar and used in the first Assembly meeting in 1620.

Initially it was required that to qualify to vote a citizen must own one share (twenty-five acres) of the Bermuda Company. This was soon changed to require ownership of land valued at two hundred pounds or more. Only men over twenty-one were entitled to vote. Parliamentary elections were held over a three-day period to allow all voters time to travel to the polling places in their parishes.

Bermuda's Government Today

Women were given the right to vote in 1944. In 1963 a Parliamentary Election Act gave the voting privilege to everyone over the age of twenty-five and allowed property owners an extra, or «plus», vote. This act was amended in 1966 when every citizen of Bermuda twenty-one years old or older was enfranchised and the plus vote was eliminated. British subjects who have resided on the islands for three years or more can also vote.

Today the islands are governed under the Constitution of 1968. The governor, appointed by the Crown for a term of three to five years, is

Commander-in-Chief of Bermuda. Bermuda's Parliament consists of a lower house, the House of Assembly, and an upper house, the Senate. Members of the House of Assembly are elected. The governor must then send for the majority party leader and ask him to form a government. The government leader recommends the members of the Cabinet and they are formally appointed by the governor. The Senate is also composed of members appointed by the governor, five on the advice of the majority leader, three on the advice of the leader of the opposition, and three chosen by the governor, a change from the former four, two and five.

The constitution contains a Bill of Rights protecting the basic rights and freedoms of individuals. The Civil Service is a nonpolitical body. There is a Supreme Court of Bermuda, from which appeals may be taken to the Court of Appeal for Bermuda. Minor offenses and traffic violations are tried in three lower courts over which magistrates preside.

Envoi

The land, the sea, and the air of Bermuda are saturated with a very special and individual beauty. The history of the islands enhances their charm and reveals that the great events of olden days did not pass this land by. Bermuda was very much involved in wars, blockade running, privateering, submarine pursuit. But for a long time now, the economy has been based on a most peaceful and pleasant industry – playing host to visitors. Time does not dim Bermuda's charms for tourists, because Bermudians bring to the art of hospitality such long experience.

THE RAILWAY TRAIL

Bermuda had a brief flirt with railways. A narrow-gauge rail line was built in the 1920s linking the entire island, and gasoline engines pulled small trains from one small station (often a corrugated iron shack) to another. In 1945 it was decided that the cost of repairing the railway after the Second World War, when maintenance had been deferred, was too great, and the tracks and rolling stock were sold to Guyana while the bus system was instituted instead.

The right-of-way was neglected for many years, except in Southampton and Somerset, where a walking, cycling and equestrian path demonstrated a beneficial use. Finally Bermuda took up the challenge, and completed, as far as possible, «The Railway Trail». The Trail is mostly reserved for walkers, horse-back riders and pedal cyclists, and provides a level pathway (apart from dips and diversions where bridges were) to enjoy a close-up acquaintance with Bermuda. Here and there are beautiful views across the water, while in other places the route passes through leafy tunnels in stretches of woodland. Part of the trail has a tarred finish, while other sections are sandy paths.

Pamphlets describing the Trail, as well as other walks, are available.

Index

Index of Color Pictures